ALAMANCE COMMUNITY COLLEGE
P.O. BOX 8000
GRAHAM, NC 27253-8000

KAYE GIBBONS

Critical Companions to Popular Contemporary Writers
Second Series

KAYE GIBBONS

A Critical Companion

Mary Jean DeMarr

CRITICAL COMPANIONS TO POPULAR CONTEMPORARY WRITERS
Kathleen Gregory Klein, Series Editor

Greenwood Press
Westport, Connecticut • London

Thanks, as always, to Kathy Klein, for including me in this project and to Lynn Malloy for her great patience. Thanks also to John Sherman for accurate and timely library research work.

Library of Congress Cataloging-in-Publication Data

DeMarr, Mary Jean, 1932–
    Kaye Gibbons : a critical companion / Mary Jean DeMarr.
        p. cm.—(Critical companions to popular contemporary writers, ISSN 1082–4979)
    Includes bibliographical references and index.
    ISBN 0–313–31933–2 (alk. paper)
        1. Gibbons, Kaye, 1960—Criticism and interpretation.   2. Women and
    literature—Southern States—History—20th century.   3. Southern States—In literature.
    I. Title.   II. Series.
    PS3557.I13917Z68   2003
    813'.54—dc21   2002032071

British Library Cataloguing in Publication Data is available.

Library of Congress Catalog Card Number: 2002032071
ISBN: 0–313–31933–2
ISSN: 1082–4979

First published in 2003

Greenwood Press, 88 Post Road West, Westport, CT 06881
An imprint of Greenwood Publishing Group, Inc.
www.greenwood.com

Printed in the United States of America

The paper used in this book complies with the
Permanent Paper Standard issued by the National
Information Standards Organization (Z39.48–1984).

10 9 8 7 6 5 4 3 2 1

In memory of the women of a Midwestern family saga:
Sarah Jane McNary Thomson
Jessie Lena Thomson Shauman
Laura Alice Shauman Bailey

ADVISORY BOARD

Contents

Series Foreword

The authors who appear in the series Critical Companions to Popular Contemporary Writers are all best-selling writers. They do not simply have one successful novel, but a string of them. Fans, critics, and specialist readers eagerly anticipate their next book. For some, high cash advances and breakthrough sales figures are automatic; movie deals often follow. Some writers become household names, recognized by almost everyone.

But, their novels are read one by one. Each reader chooses to start and, more importantly, to finish a book because of what she or he finds there. The real test of a novel is in the satisfaction its readers experience. This series acknowledges the extraordinary involvement of readers and writers in creating a best-seller.

The authors included in this series were chosen by an Advisory Board composed of high school English teachers and high school and public librarians. They ranked a list of best-selling writers according to their popularity among different groups of readers. For the first series, writers in the top-ranked group who had received no book-length, academic, literary analysis (or none in at least the past ten years) were chosen. Because of this selection method, Critical Companions to Popular Contemporary Writers meets a need that is being addressed nowhere else. The success of these volumes as reported by reviewers, librarians, and teachers led to an expansion of the series mandate to include some writers with wide critical attention—Toni Morrison, John Irving, and Maya Angelou, for example—to extend the usefulness of the series.

The volumes in the series are written by scholars with particular expertise in analyzing popular fiction. These specialists add an academic focus to the popular success that these writers already enjoy.

The series is designed to appeal to a wide range of readers. The general reading public will find explanations for the appeal of these well-known writers. Fans will find biographical and fictional questions answered. Students will find literary analysis, discussions of fictional genres, carefully organized introductions to new ways of reading the novels, and bibliographies for additional research. Whether browsing through the book for pleasure or using it for an assignment, readers will find that the most recent novels of the authors are included.

Each volume begins with a biographical chapter drawing on published information, autobiographies or memoirs, prior interviews, and, in some cases, interviews given especially for this series. A chapter on literary history and genres describes how the author's work fits into a larger literary context. The following chapters analyze the writer's most important, most popular, and most recent novels in detail. Each chapter focuses on one or more novels. This approach, suggested by the advisory board as the most useful to student research, allows for an in-depth analysis of the writer's fiction. Close and careful readings with numerous examples show readers exactly how the novels work. These chapters are organized around three central elements: plot development (how the story line moves forward), character development (what the reader knows of the important figures), and theme (the significant ideas of the novel). Chapters may also include sections on generic conventions (how the novel is similar to or different from others in its same category of science fiction, fantasy, thriller, etc.), narrative point of view (who tells the story and how), symbols and literary language, and historical or social context. Each chapter ends with an "alternative reading" of the novel. The volume concludes with a primary and secondary bibliography, including reviews.

The alternative readings are a unique feature of this series. By demonstrating a particular way of reading each novel, they provide a clear example of how a specific perspective can reveal important aspects of the book. In the alternative reading sections, one contemporary literary theory—way of reading, such as feminist criticism, Marxism, new historicism, deconstruction, or Jungian psychological critique—is defined in brief, easily comprehensible language. That definition is then applied to the novel to highlight specific features that might go unnoticed or be understood differently in a more general reading. Each volume defines two or three specific theories, making them part of the reader's understanding of how diverse meanings may be constructed from a single novel.

Taken collectively, the volumes in the Critical Companions to Popular Contemporary Writers series provide a wide-ranging investigation of the complexities of current best-selling fiction. By treating these novels seriously as both literary works and publishing successes, the series demonstrates the potential of popular literature in contemporary culture.

Kathleen Gregory Klein
Southern Connecticut State University

1

Kaye Gibbons: Life and Works

A lifelong North Carolinian who has found her voice by speaking in the voices of many strong North Carolina women, Kaye Gibbons has reached a worldwide audience. In her concentration upon the place and people she knows well, she has managed to speak to and for people who have never seen her own place. Strong elements of autobiography appear in several of her novels, but these stories also achieve universality. Her passion for language enables her to give authenticity to her characters, and their pluck, perseverance, and courage in the face of occasionally terrible troubles make them admirable as well as believable. She has accomplished the sometimes difficult feat of producing fiction which is both best-selling and respected by critics.

PERSONAL DETAILS

Kaye Batts was born on May 5, 1960, in Wilson, North Carolina, to a tobacco farmer named Charles Batts and his wife Alice. The family's home was in a rural Nash County community called Bend of the River, which is south of Rocky Mount, North Carolina. Careful readers will recognize Bend of the River and Rocky Mount as important locations in Gibbons's fiction. She has several siblings, a brother thirteen years older and a sister nine years older than she. Her family is an old one in the area and is related to Nathaniel Batts, who has been described as the "first-known permanent white settler in North Carolina," having established himself on the coast in 1655 (Mason 1993, 156).

The family was poor as the future author was growing up, and readers may imagine what it was like for them from the depictions given in *Ellen Foster* and *A Virtuous Woman*, the two novels which are most directly based on that experience. However, as decisive as her immersion in the culture and life of the rural people were the tragedies which befell her family when she was between ten and thirteen years old. Her mother apparently suffered from manic depression (now more usually called bipolar disorder), the same disorder which has afflicted the writer. Mrs. Batts killed herself in 1970 at the relatively young age of forty-seven by taking an overdose of sleeping pills. Gibbons had loved and admired her mother greatly, for the mother was a strong woman who was responsible for the family's stability, and the child missed her deeply. As an adult sufferer from manic depression, she has expressed sympathy for her mother, whose illness occurred before lithium, fluoxetine, and other medications became available (Powell 1994, 123). After the mother's death, the young Gibbons lived with her father for a time, becoming responsible for handling all the practical details of their daily lives, until he drank himself to death. This story, of course, strongly resembles the experience of Ellen Foster, the narrator and protagonist as well as the title character of Gibbons's first novel.

And the similarity does not end there. In these troubled years, she briefly lived with an aunt, her mother's sister, and then moved to a foster home which "she had chosen partly on the basis of observing at church the woman whose home it was" (Mason 1993, 156–57). Here, readers will recognize the happy ending of *Ellen Foster*. Her own story, however, continued, for she lived with several other relatives in turn, and finally, after her older brother's marriage, she moved in with him and his new wife in their home in Rocky Mount. These later events do not figure in the fiction, perhaps because they would be anticlimactic after the solution of moving in with the foster family brought her character to the stability she had sought. In a 1993 interview, Gibbons herself is quoted as summing up the similarities between herself and Ellen, acknowledging that the novel is "emotionally autobiographical" and going on to say that her "mother *did* commit suicide when I was 10" and that her father "really did drink himself to death. But I didn't go to live with my grandmother, as Ellen does, although I did live with a couple of aunts before moving in with my older brother, which was fortunate for me. But the years between 10 and 13 were pretty hard" (Summer 1993, 60).

The rest of her formative years were less eventful, certainly less traumatic, but they do reveal other very important similarities to her character. She was a bookish youngster, discovering early the love of reading, and she began writing poetry quite young. For her, school was a kind of refuge, for there she found a number of things that were very important to her—order and discipline among them, as well as the stimulation of learning. After her public school years ended, she attended North Carolina State University on a Veterans Administration scholarship, also working at the university library there. Eventually transferring to the University of North Carolina at Chapel Hill, she changed majors several times, from political science to history, before finally concentrating in English.

However, she did not graduate, for her own manic-depressive mental illness intervened. She spent the months from August 1981 to March 1982 in a hospital in Raleigh but was able to attend classes during this time. In this general period she also met and married her first husband, Michael Gibbons, who was a graduate student in landscape architecture when they met. She has retained his last name as her pen name after their divorce, doubtless because her first fame, achieved with the publication of her first two novels, occurred during their marriage.

They were married on May 12, 1984, and their first daughter, Mary, was born the following year. Two other daughters, Leslie and Louise, followed in 1987 and 1989. Attentive readers will recognize that Gibbons has given their names to the children of the protagonist of *On the Occasion of My Last Afternoon*. Meanwhile, in the summer of 1985, another momentous event occurred, as Gibbons took a course in Southern literature from Louis Rubin, a well-known professor and critic. Here she read a number of authors from her region and recognized authentic voices speaking in ways which spoke deeply to her. Several months after the course ended, she began a manuscript which she showed to Rubin. With his encouragement, she finished it; the result was *Ellen Foster*, which Rubin then had published by his firm, Algonquin Books, of Chapel Hill. After its remarkable impact, unusual for a first novel, Gibbons has moved from success to success as an author. Rubin has remained an inspiration and an encouragement to her.

Meanwhile, her life went on. She has continued to struggle with her manic-depressive illness, controlling her mood swings with medication. The disease is characterized by variations from periods of depression in which the patient has trouble functioning and may withdraw from human interaction to periods of dramatically elevated activity and excitement in which the patient may feel almost superhuman and have illusions of power and insights. In between, there may be times of normal functioning. In a 1995 interview, she indicated that she had at one time taken twenty-seven pills a day for mood control but was at that time requiring only nineteen (O'Briant 1995). She has said that she writes best when in a state of "hypomania," a condition between normality and mania in which the excitement of mania is somewhat controlled by the underlying normality but creativity is energized by the mania (Powell 1994, 128). But those times, however productive they may be, are also "like living without a net" (Powell 1994, 128). In that "in-between state," Gibbons says, "it's like looking out of a very clear window and seeing the story on the other side. I have a hypersensitivity to language, and my thoughts come easily in an organized, patterned way" (Powell 1994, 128). She considers herself fortunate to be one of the few persons suffering from manic depression to be able to "stay in charge" (Powell 1994, 123), but she does not take lithium, finding that it deadens her sensations (Powell 1994, 128). Her illness is, she has said, "a curse and a gift, and I have to endure the episodes to write" (Powell 1994, 131).

Her first marriage ended in the early 1990s, with enough anger that she planned to remove Gibbons's name from the dedication of new printings of *A Virtuous Woman* and replace it with the name of her second husband (Malinowski 1995). She remarried on September 25, 1993. Her second marriage, to Frank P. Ward, an attorney in Raleigh, has brought two stepchildren and a settled home into her life. She describes her husband as remarkably supportive and understanding.

North Carolina has been her home for all of her life, with only two significant excursions away, one to California and one to New York, both brief and both immediately realized as mistakes. Unlike those authors who find themselves able to call up their native places only when they achieve distance from them, she apparently can receive nourishment only from her homeland. The sources for all of her fiction come from her own experience and her own places.

PROFESSIONAL LIFE AND REPUTATION

Six novels, of remarkably consistently high quality, characterize Gibbons's career. The first, *Ellen Foster* (1987), was rapidly written at a young age and is the most directly and obviously autobiographical of her books. Ellen's story is very much like her own in many details. Oddly perhaps, it actually began not as fiction narrated by the character who so much resembles herself but as a poem narrated by a young African American girl. After revision, Gibbons realized that the proper voice for the book was that of its young white protagonist, and the black girl was transmuted into the character of Starletta; the poem essentially disappeared, and the remaining remnants (Jordan 1993, 68–69) would not be noticed by readers. Comments made in a much later interview, in 1995 upon the publication of *Sights Unseen*, suggest how very close to Gibbons herself Ellen is in some details as well as in general history. Speaking of her own happy home with her second husband, she said, "It's hard to go from living a hardscrabble life on Bend of the River Road to being on this street. . . . When I was a child, it was very important that I grow up and live in a brick house. . . . because the children who lived in brick houses had responsible parents who didn't drink" (O'Briant 1995). Ellen, like her creator, makes life in a brick house a symbolic ambition, and like her creator she achieves this fate, for the foster mother of her happy ending does indeed live in a brick house. Gibbons did, for a time, however, attempt to conceal these similarities, claiming that Ellen was completely fictitious and that her experiences were in no way those of the author. To readers, however, this is unimportant, for Ellen is believably human and appealing in her own right, and, for enjoyment of the novel, her sources in the author's experience are irrelevant.

After Gibbons showed thirty pages of a rough draft of the novel to Rubin and received his encouragement to continue, she wrote *Ellen Foster* quickly, not even finding it necessary to do much editing or rewriting. The experience of writing out this part of her own life was both energizing and draining, but it taught her that writing was what she now wanted to do for a living. Interestingly, technique was a concern for her even in the writing of this very personal book. For example, she consciously dispensed with the use of most punctuation, because she "wanted to see if I could make the voice gradations and the changes so obvious without them that they were unnecessary. I really made a conscious choice" (Gretlund 2000, 141). Even from the beginning of her career, her craft has been important to her, perhaps nearly as important as her subject matter.

For a first novel published by a small regional press, *Ellen Foster* was surprisingly reviewed to consistent and wide enthusiastic acclaim. Her language, characterization, and sense of narration were highly praised, and she was compared to such writers as Mark Twain, Eudora Welty, J.D. Salinger, and Anne Tyler. The novel sold well, and it has never been out of print in the fifteen years since its publication. It won several prizes,

including the Sue Kaufman Prize for First Fiction from the American
Academy and Institute of Arts and Letters and a special citation from
the Ernest Hemingway Foundation. Eventually it was made into a television movie, in 1997, and, with her second novel, became a selection
for Oprah's Book Club in that same year. Sometimes considered a book
for young adults, it has also reached a wide readership among adults;
sometimes summed up as a "regional" or "Southern" novel, it has never
lacked for appreciation outside of that region. It was indeed an auspi-
cious beginning for her career.

Gibbons's second novel, *A Virtuous Woman*, which was published two
years after the first in 1989, again by Algonquin, was inescapably compared and contrasted with *Ellen Foster* because of the great success of
that first novel. Although clearly related, the two novels, however, do
differ in significant ways. The second book lacks the obviously autobiographical character of the first while having essentially the same setting.
The technique of the first-person narrator, so ably handled through Ellen
in the first novel, is both used and varied. Here Gibbons employs two
separate narrators, alternating their tales and skillfully differentiating
their voices. Instead of the story of a young girl growing up, this is the
tale of a marriage.

This book was considerably more difficult for Gibbons to write, doubtless because of its greater distance from her own experience, and it eventually went through four drafts. Like its predecessor, however, it was
warmly received by critics and readers, and it, too, has remained in print
until the present. Reviewers commented that it lived up to the promise
of Gibbons's first novel and indicated that this was indeed a novelist to
watch, not a one-book author whose potential is written out after a first,
autobiographical, work. Although some reviewers were puzzled or troubled by certain aspects of its narrative method and structure, others
praised both aspects of the book. Some classified Gibbons as a woman's
writer and commented on her women as being both better characterized
and more sympathetic than her men. Once again, Gibbons's language,
her ability to convey colloquial speech, and her sense of place were com-
mended, as was her ability to balance humor and pain. For this novel,
she was awarded a National Endowment for the Arts Fellowship.

Gibbons's next two novels are inextricably linked to each other, since
each is a multigenerational family saga tracing the experiences of several
generations of women. *A Cure for Dreams* (1991) and *Charms for the Easy
Life* (1993) both cover a period which can be broadly described as the
first third or half of the twentieth century, and both use the perspective

of the lives and experiences of successions of mothers and daughters living in rural North Carolina and gradually improving their lives over this period. Both novels are easily considered women's books, and each can be seen as lacking in male characters able to balance the women, although this criticism is less true of the later work. In fact, the second novel was originally intended as a sequel to the earlier one, but this linkage was quickly dropped and the two works are completely independent of each other. Pivotal for both, and for Gibbons's continued development as a writer, was her discovery of the papers of the Federal Writers Project which are held in the Southern Historical Collection of the University of North Carolina at Chapel Hill, which she credits in the acknowledgments prefacing *A Cure for Dreams*. These papers, including many interviews with many ordinary people who have lived ordinary lives through times which later were to seem extraordinary to others, showed Gibbons many varied voices and taught her much about the language and idioms of these people. She had long gloried in the language she heard about her and had been able to use it with imagination and skill in her first two novels; however, these papers enlarged her sense of people and their speech and have been crucial in her continued development as a writer. The acknowledgment page for *Charms for the Easy Life* similarly mentions the Works Progress Administration (WPA) interviews dating from the period of the Great Depression and adds her praise to the work of Studs Terkel, famous for his work in publishing his own interviews with working people. She calls those documents the "primary sources of inspiration for this novel." Always sensitive to nuances of common speech, her discovery of all these papers has helped her consciously develop her skill at depicting her characters and their times and place through their use of language.

Describing *A Cure for Dreams* as a "matriarchal history," in contrast to "most family histories" which are "patriarchal histories," Gibbons has said that she began by trying to write in an omnisicient narrative method (that is, the story being told using third-person pronouns for all characters with no character acting as teller of events, thus giving the impression of objectivity). She found, however, that this method was not working, and so she began over, returning to the first-person method which she had used in her first two books and would continue using in later works. This method does seem particularly appropriate in a writer so concerned with the voices and speech of her characters. Using it, she can allow them to speak for themselves.

Both these novels were, like her earlier work, well received by critics and readers alike. Her eye for detail, her ear for speech, and her economy of style were praised. A number of critics commented particularly on the books' reliance on strong female characters and their paucity of believable or admirable males. Gibbons's comment, above, about writing "matriarchal" as opposed to "patriarchal" history, seems relevant here, and surely she is right to insist on using her own materials, her own subject matter. And from the beginning that subject matter has been the lives of women, as one of her accomplishments has been giving voices to people, particularly women, whose voices have long been submerged. And, it must be added, this criticism of her concentration on female personages has not been strong enough to hamper her generally favorable reception. She received the Nelson Algren Heartland Award for Fiction given by the *Chicago Tribune* in 1991, and a PEN/Revson Foundation Fellowship, and a North Carolina Sir Walter Raleigh Award for *A Cure for Dreams*. Gibbons's change of publishers, from Algonquin to Putnam's, for the publication of *A Cure for Dreams*, should be noted here. The change, she has said, was amicable and made for purely professional reasons.

Continuing her pattern of a novel every two years, Gibbons published *Sights Unseen* in 1995. With this novel, she once again turned to very personal materials, including some that are obviously autobiographical. However, in this novel, imagination is more heavily blended with fact than it had been in *Ellen Foster*. *Sights Unseen* was perhaps more painful for her to write despite being more fictionalized, as a result going through as many as seven or eight drafts. Her subject here is an analysis of the manic-depressive illness with which she has lived since 1981 and which she believes she inherited from her mother. Now the mother herself of three daughters, she puzzled over both her sense of the loss of her own mother and her concern that she was, because of her own illness, not sufficiently available to her own girls. She felt that having lacked mothering in her own girlhood, and having longed desperately for it, she necessarily also lacked maternal skills and worried about the impact of all this on her own daughters. Her basic plot here, then, of a manic-depressive mother and a daughter who loves her mother and is confused by the situation, comes from Gibbons's own experience on the levels of both the mother and the daughter.

It was when *Sights Unseen* was published that the author went public with the facts of her own youth and her illness. Previously she had denied that *Ellen Foster* was autobiographical or that her mother had committed suicide. Now she not only revealed the fiction's basis in her own life but also talked openly about her own illness. She has acknowledged that this novel was particularly difficult for her to write, for both emotional and technical reasons. After an early draft was written, she realized that she really had two books in one, and she achieved a workable version only when she "split it up" (Gretlund 2000, 151). She has said that at the time of writing this novel, she had just lived through a "year-long manic depression. Out of control." As a result she "had a really fine memory of what it feels like to have that non-stop voice in the head" (Gretlund 2000, 151). She acknowledges that she is herself much like Maggie, the mother in her story, but she decided to give the narration to Hattie, the daughter, who is in some ways like that part of herself she had depicted in *Ellen Foster*.

Much like the rest of her fiction, *Sights Unseen* was published to warm reviews and wide sales. Praise for her economy of style and effective use of colloquial speech continued, although much of the discussion inevitably centered around her depiction of mental illness. Gibbons received the distinction of a special honor in France, a country in which her fiction has always been well received and widely read. She was, in 1991, named a Chevalier de l'Ordre des Arts and des Letters, making her a French knight.

On the Occasion of My Last Afternoon, published in 1998, broke new ground for Gibbons in one particularly obvious way. As a clear entry in the genre of historical fiction, it differs from all of her previous work, including *A Cure for Dreams* and *Charms for the Easy Life*, both of which had historical elements but did not fit easily into that genre. Even more obviously than in the two earlier, semihistorical works, research was important in the writing of this novel. Again, however, the research was not used to give her a subject, but rather enabled her to develop a subject already meaningful to her. Here, however, she has said the research came close to taking over. She had consulted a number of primary sources which gave her examples of the voices of actual Southern women who had lived through the American Civil War (diaries, letters, and the like) and become fascinated by the details of their experiences and daily lives, so much so that she finally had to rewrite, making sure that the details of the period were integrated into the narrative, remaining accurate but always there for a purpose in developing character or plot (O'Briant 1998). In doing research, she had stayed away from later books about the period, those which she calls "revisionist, politically correct books" (O'Briant 1998) in order to avoid imposing late-twentieth-century propaganda upon her story. She has said that her research taught her a great deal about the strength and courage, the toughness of the women of this period, and these characteristics are, as a result, notable in her central character.

It must be noted that even though this new book differs in an obvious way from those which preceded it, it also shows great continuity with Gibbons's earlier work. Setting and use of first-person narrative, along with the centrality of women characters and women's issues, bear the familiar hallmarks of her fiction. Structure, while more nearly chronological than sometimes in earlier books, remains functional, serving the purposes of the revelation of plot and character rather than controlling them as happens in some historical novels which follow a strictly time-oriented story line.

Once again this novel was widely and in general favorably reviewed. Negative comments, as in the evaluations of her novels, tended to concentrate on her male characters, suggesting that they tend to be less believable than her women, that they are too often stick-figures, not complex mixtures of good and evil as her women are. Previously, some critics had commented on the lack of strong and admirable male characters in her work, but in the case of this latest book, some were dismayed that the husband of the protagonist is too perfect, too idealized. Earlier parts of the novel, particularly the gripping opening scene, were highly lauded, with some reviewers finding later portions of the work less absorbing. Similarly, some found the central character more interesting and believable as a young girl than in her later years. Several reviewers, in fact, would seem not to have completed reading the novel or to have read it carelessly (one ignoring its depiction of the Civil War, in fact, writing as if it were a novel about the prewar South). Almost unanimously, however, reviewers praised her uses of details and skill at integrating those details into the daily lives of her characters, so that they re-create the period for readers unobtrusively, without calling attention to themselves as period details but rather being simply a part of the fabric of the characters' experience.

2

Genres and Patterns

Gibbons's fiction does not conform to any one of the genres of popular fiction, such as thrillers, detective novels, romances, and the like. However, several of her books do fit into particular genres, and readers will observe a number of patterns which persist through some, or in a few cases, all of her work. Most notable are the consistency of her use of Southern, in particular North Carolina, settings and her employment of the first-person narrative of strong women. In fact, her work has from the first been categorized as belonging to the important strand of "Southern women's fiction." This places her in good company, with writers such as Elizabeth Madox Roberts, Kate Chopin, Zora Neale Hurston, Eudora Welty, Alice Walker, Flannery O'Connor, Carson McCullers, Rita Mae Brown, Lee Smith, and many others. These are all writers, like Gibbons, who are firmly rooted in their place and who find their materials in the lives of ordinary people who contend with the effects of the particular history of their region. Southern fiction has been perhaps the most prolific and rich of the regional American literatures, owing partly to a common sense of history and a culture based in the South's bloody past. Those elements of history most powerful in their influence have been the effects of slavery and its violent abolition and the often romanticized but bitter defeat in a bloody civil war. Poverty, racial relations, and, particularly among white middle-class people, a sense of the loss of a special way of life continue to affect and enrich the fiction coming from this area.

Women writers of the area have long insisted on the particular strength and endurance of women, both white and black—black women who lived through the experience of slavery, and white women who maintained the integrity of their families through the suffering of the Civil War and the bitter poverty which followed. For many of these writers, language is central, a women's idiom rich in colloquialisms and expressive of the lives and experiences they have come through. Southern spoken dialect and cadences remain immediately identifiable to Americans from other regions, and that spoken language, conveyed on the printed page, adds richness and authenticity to the prose of these women writers.

Kaye Gibbons, a lifelong resident of North Carolina, belongs comfortably with these Southern women writers, by reason of the type and quality of her work, not just by the accident of her birth. She has so far used only first-person narrators, characters who tell their own stories in their own dialects and who are as steeped in their culture and folkways as she is herself. Interestingly, she for some time attempted to make her settings universal by not specifying them, from a kind of sense of regional inferiority. She has admitted, "I wanted not to set my novels anywhere. I didn't think that my little postage stamp of space was worthy of literature. . . . *Ellen Foster* was set nowhere" (Powell 1994, 129). Only with her fourth novel, *Charms for the Easy Life*, she went on to say, did she begin to write fiction "with a somewhere to it," and since that was successful, she was willing to continue giving her stories identifiable locales. However, it is doubtful that any reader was confused about the locale of any of her fiction, including *Ellen Foster*. Language and idiom, customs and folkways, the general tone and temper of the novel and those which followed clearly indicated a setting in the Southeast region of the United States.

In discussing Gibbons's fiction, a number of critics have commented on the importance of talk, of language, to her and her characters, and on how typical this emphasis is for Southern writers, especially Southern women writers. Gibbons reveals this concern most obviously in her choice of first-person narrative method, allowing her protagonists to speak for themselves, in their own idioms, sometimes ungrammatical and often full of Southern dialectal turns of speech. This use of colloquial language of her region was natural in her first two books, although it was also clearly conscious and intentional. By the time she began writing *A Cure for Dreams*, her third book, she had discovered the papers of the Federal Writers Project, deposited in the Southern Historical Collection of the University of North Carolina at Chapel Hill, a discovery that was to be very important for all of her remaining work. That novel, in fact, bears an epigram taken from W.T. Couch, identified as "Regional Director" of that project, who is quoted as saying, "With all our talk of democracy it seems not inappropriate to let the people speak for themselves." In those papers she read—and heard—the language of ordinary people speaking about ordinary lives, and from them she learned how to transmute their language into the voices of the characters she was yet to create. She found in them odd or unusual turns of phrase as she learned about their lives and experiences.

A Cure for Dreams, in fact, might be considered a kind of turning point in this regard, for in this novel Gibbons makes talk an important theme, perhaps even the basis of the novel. The framing narrator, in introducing her mother, who will tell the major part of the novel, emphasizes how the mother talked and how the daughter had spent her life listening, summing it up by saying, *"Talking was my mother's life"* (1). The mother "talks" the novel, telling the story of her life, and in the process telling the stories of other women as well. Fittingly, the framing narrator also closes the book emphasizing this strand, describing her own first true memory as being *"the sounds of the women talking"* (171).

For her remaining novels, Gibbons continued this reliance on women's voices and her use of research, of studying the authentic stories of real women told in their own voices, to give reality to her own characters. These other novels, however, are less explicit than *A Cure for Dreams* in making talk and storytelling actual themes. Nevertheless, the Southern love of a good yarn and delight in a well-told tale, conveyed naturally and in the speech of the place, are basic to the texture of all these books.

Beyond her identification as a writer of Southern women's fiction, Gibbons has not been particularly identified with any of the popular genres; several of her novels do relate to particular literary forms. *Ellen Foster* and, to a lesser extent, *Sights Unseen* may be examined as maturation novels; *A Cure for Dreams* and *Charms for the Easy Life* are family sagas; and *On the Occasion of My Last Afternoon* is a historical novel.

GENRES

Maturation Novel

The genre often referred to as the "maturation novel" also goes by other labels: "Education novel," "initiation novel," or the German name "Bildungsroman" are some of the more familiar. Although there may be some distinctions between their exact meanings, in general all these terms refer to fiction in which a protagonist, generally a young person who begins as naïve or ignorant, learns through her or his experiences many things necessary for successful functioning in the adult world and achieves a realistic understanding of what that world is like, bringing disillusioning experiences which teach an awareness of the evils to be contended with. A well-known example, one with which *Ellen Foster* has often been compared, is Mark Twain's *The Adventures of Huckleberry Finn*.

Some novels, "failed education novels," more pessimistic, reveal a protagonist whose experiences are negative in their impact and lead to withdrawal or defeat. Many stories with female protagonists exemplify this form, reminding readers of the cultural difficulties faced by women who attempt to become truly mature and autonomous. In so doing, they often must choose between fulfilling the expected feminine roles and becoming strong adults; too often they decide to subordinate themselves to others. Gibbons, always an optimist, develops successful maturation experiences for her characters. It is significant to note here that the two novels which relate to this genre are her two novels most closely bound up with her own personal experience.

Ellen Foster fits neatly into this category. The title character is a young person who undergoes a great many experiences which demonstrate for her the evils of the world and of humankind. She sees her mother abused by her father, loses the mother to suicide, sees her father drink himself into oblivion and resists his attempts to abuse her, lives with relatives who neglect and ignore her, undergoes poverty and deprivation, and discovers in herself the irrationality of race prejudice. Although she could never be called naïve, she certainly learns and grows from her observations and experiences. Partly this is a result of a few good experiences and observations which balance against her initiation into evil: her friendship with a young black girl, the warmth of that youngster's family, and her brief stay in the home of a nurturing teacher are crucial here. Partly, however, it is a result of her very character, for from the beginning she is depicted as being spunky and courageous, determined to survive and make something of herself.

Ellen's success in winning through all her maturing experiences is emphasized in two ways. On a plot level, she is shown as achieving a happy living situation, with a foster mother who will love and care for her, the opposite of what she had found with various family members. And this living situation is one which she finds for herself, so her accomplishment of this happy ending is emblematic of her success. Second, on a thematic level, she achieves self-knowledge, especially about her racist attitudes. She had felt superior to her young black friend, but she finally realizes how meaningless and cruel those feelings were, and she humbles herself by apologizing to the friend. Her emotional and mental maturity are revealed by this behavior. *Ellen Foster* is a good example, in all these ways, of a female maturation novel showing a successful initiation process.

Less neatly fitting into the category of maturation novel is Gibbons's fifth book, *Sights Unseen*. The focus of this novel is doubled, as the stories of two principal characters, a mother and a daughter, are developed. The mother suffers from a severe mental illness, and the daughter attempts to cope with and understand the effects of the illness on her mother and on herself and the family. The daughter narrates the story, and her narrative presents its materials as if they were about the mother. However, the daughter's own story emerges through her telling. The novel, therefore, may be seen in two ways, as a story of a woman's mental illness and its final successful treatment or as a story of the growing up of a young girl who is deprived of her mother because of that mother's mental disease. When examined in this second light, *Sights Unseen* may be interpreted as a story of maturation.

The daughter, Hattie, takes readers through her life story, up until the time at which her mother undergoes treatment for her illness, but although the narrative proper stops with that event, Hattie mentions briefly some events from later years. Through the story of Hattie's youth as the daughter of a manic-depressive, Hattie's maturation into life is depicted. Through her descriptions of the mother's later death and her own professional training as a physician and motherhood, the success of her maturation process is demonstrated.

It might be argued that the evils into which Hattie is initiated are really problems caused by the bad luck of her mother's illness and not really significant to the nature of the world in which she will have to live. This is a reasonable argument, but it is also true that the dynamics of her family and their ways of coping with the mother's illness do give her windows into the adult world. Her tyrannical grandfather, her brother's sibling rivalry with her, and the malice and silliness of some of the other characters are revealed as a result of the stress under which the mother's condition places the family. Nevertheless, *Sights Unseen*, although not really a very clear example of that form, does qualify in some respects as a maturation novel.

Family Saga

Two novels, written one after the other in the middle of Gibbons's career, are similar to each other in showing characteristics that place them in a genre which might be called the "family saga." This genre may be briefly defined as including fiction which follows the stories of several members of an extended family, either as that family develops through several generations or as it branches out into a number of related nuclear families. Among the most famous practitioners of this genre, Galsworthy (with his Forsyte Saga) and Faulkner might be mentioned. Faulkner, like Gibbons a Southern writer, has written novels which belong in both types of this genre. *Absalom, Absalom!* and *The Sound and the Fury* both follow the experiences and fates of members of prominent families in his world of Yoknapatawpha County in Mississippi over several generations, showing how the actions of earlier members of the family impinge on the lives of their descendants. Snopes family members, consisting of a variety of cousins, even some rather distantly related, are presented in three novels, *The Hamlet*, *The Town*, and *The Mansion*. The impact on their community of the often unscrupulous behavior of members of this clan is developed. Gibbons's two family sagas are of the type which follows a family through time, the multigenerational saga.

A Cure for Dreams and *Charms for the Easy Life* both follow a maternal, or female, line of descent through three (or, in the case of the earlier novel, a fourth with less emphasis and development than her descendants) generations. In both books, there is a strong emphasis on the relationships of the mother-daughter pairs, particularly on the ways in which the younger characters are nurtured by and learn from their mothers. The second novel also emphasizes strongly the relationship of the grandmother and granddaughter, depicting the way in which this younger woman is encouraged and taught by her grandmother. Both novels, then, develop worlds which are largely female, in which males often appear only briefly and are often characterized in unfavorable ways. The central female characters, while placing great importance on their family relationships, find meaning and continuity in their connections with other women, not generally with the men in their lives.

Female relationships, however, expand in these books, especially in *A Cure for Dreams*, beyond those of blood. That novel emphasizes the creation, with the leadership of one of them, of a community of women which supports and enriches their lives. The women of the central family reach out to other women and, in fact, are able to lead some of their friends through crises in their lives. Additionally, when one of the central women finds disappointment in her experiences away from her community, she returns home to her mother and friends to rebuild her life.

Both novels reveal Gibbons's persistent optimism, for both demonstrate improvement through time of the situations of the family members. The women of the earlier generations in both stories come from situations of poverty and ignorance. In each case, the woman who becomes a matriarch leaves her birth home after she is married in order to build a new and better life. In each case, her husband proves unsatisfactory, and in her new life she concentrates upon her daughter or upon her own adventures and growth. In the earlier novel, Lottie goes about creating a community of women, and Charlie Kate in the later one builds upon her knowledge of midwifery and folk healing to become an accepted member of the medical world of her new town. Both novels follow the experiences of the central families through the first third or more of the twentieth century, tracing in general terms the economic, technological, or political changes of the times and paralleling those changes with the gradual improvement in the status and class or status of the women themselves. The youngest women, the granddaughters, are left as young adults with fine prospects, far better than were presented to either their mothers or grandmothers, and hints are given in each case that their lives will be easier than those of their forebears.

These two novels are a bit unusual among family sagas in making use of complex methods of first-person narration and in employing structures which are only loosely chronological. In each case, Gibbons has complicated her presentation of her materials by selecting techniques which enable her to focus her themes and characterizations and which pull the reader into her stories, making them in some senses her collaborators. Readers see events through the women's eyes, and they learn information about their experiences in an order which is sometimes based on a kind of association of ideas, not simply their order in time, and so the readers must piece them together. These devices not only add complexity to the narrative, but also they enrich the stories and their meanings. Relatively short as family sagas go, these two novels are nevertheless complex and interesting examples of the genre.

Historical Novel

Gibbons's most recent book, *On the Occasion of My Last Afternoon*, is an obvious example of a historical novel. That genre may simply be described as fiction set in the past which makes use of historical events or personages. However, the genre is also a varied one. At one end of its range are thinly disguised but accurate recountings of actual events, including actual historical figures, in which much of the interest and attention are directed to the history itself. Sometimes names are not even changed. At the other end are works in which no or few historical figures are present and in which purely imagined characters live out their lives against the backdrop of historical events, with the interest being in the experiences of the characters and the historical materials of subordinate interest. Such novels, no less than their counterparts at the opposite end of the range within the genre, may be meticulously researched and accurate. The point is simply that the historical materials are used for different purposes and in different ways.

On the Occasion of My Last Afternoon is a novel of the second type, in which the primary interest is on the characters as they live through their historical period more than in the history itself. Events such as the occurrence of Civil War battles and the like are mentioned and directly affect the action of the novel, but they are not directly depicted. The more important elements of history are cultural and social, with strong presentations of the violence often present in early nineteenth-century American society and, especially, of slavery and the relations between white middle-class or aristocratic families and the African Americans who served them. Gibbons studied historical sources and attempted to make her text accurate, especially in the language of her characters. The way of life of people in mid-nineteenth-century North Carolina, especially in the periods before and during the war, is presented as seen through the eyes of an intelligent and sensitive young woman, and it is the nature of this way of life which probably makes the strongest impression upon most readers. They would not go to this novel to learn about the chronology or the technology of the war, but they are likely to come away from the novel with an increased feeling for the texture of the society and culture and for the sufferings and the triumphs of characters like those she depicts.

PATTERNS

Readers are most apt to be drawn to Gibbons's fiction by her characters, her settings, her language, and her humor. The novels tend to re-
semble each other in all these ways, so a reader who enjoys one of the
books is likely to enjoy the others. In addition to these qualities, a reader
who follows the fiction through the six novels so far published will observe a number of additional patterns which are repeated from novel to
novel, sometimes in all the books and sometimes in a few. These range
from the very trivial, such as the repeated presence of an African-
American female character bearing the name of Mavis, to the very important such as the use of first-person narratives or the depiction of
unequal marriages. For illustrative purposes, it may be helpful to examine several of these patterns. Some particularly important patterns,
because they are developed elsewhere, will not be scrutinized here.
These include the aforementioned use of first-person narrative, the presence of North Carolina settings, the centrality of strong, female protagonists, and the use of doubled narrative voices or perspective prominent
in *A Virtuous Woman, A Cure for Dreams, Charms for the Easy Life*, and
Sights Unseen.

Unequal Marriages

This plot motif appears in several forms. In the first two novels, *Ellen
Foster* and *A Virtuous Woman*, the inequality between marriage partners
is one of class or status, and in the first, but not the second, of these
books the inequality leads to disaster. In *Ellen Foster*, Ellen's mother has
"married down" in status. Coming from a propertied, middle-class family, she has married a poor man. Even more important than their inequality in class and wealth but related to it is their inequality in
education and culture. Ellen's father is a sometimes violent alcoholic, and
he is deeply resentful of her family's rejection of him. The reasons for
his deep anger, even hatred, and his drinking are not given, but they
may be related to his military service, which is only hinted at. His behavior might seem to fit into the pattern displayed by many veterans of
the Vietnam War, and it is worth noting that Gibbons's own father, presumably the model for him, was himself a veteran of military service.
His character is more significant than any explanation of motivation in
defining the inequality of these partners, for he is not only alcoholic and

poor but also an abuser of his wife and daughter and a vituperative racist. His wife, on the other hand, is a gentle and sensitive soul, who deeply loves their daughter but is defeated by the situation into which her marriage has placed her. When illness intervenes, she is unable to cope with her husband's cruelty, and her suicide is the result.

Quite different is the use of this motif in *A Virtuous Woman*. The principal marriage depicted in this second novel is similar in yoking a gently reared middle-class young woman with a poor, lower-class husband. Similarly, he is a hard drinker, but his drinking is not so out of control as that of Ellen's father. Added to the inequalities presented here is a great difference in age: the husband is approximately twice as old as his wife. As in the first novel, the wife's illness intervenes, but the result is quite different. Although husband and wife meet this crisis quite differently, the love that has earlier allowed them to build a loving and lasting partnership carries them through. He lacks the sensitivity to give her the emotional support she longs for in her last days, but she is sure of his love, and her understanding prevails. Her care for him throughout their marriage continues even after her death, because of her preparation of enough food for him to last until, she hopes, he is over his first grief at losing her. This unequal marriage, despite its flaws, is truly successful. Thus it is an obvious exception to Gibbons's usual development of this pattern. However, another marriage, briefly shown and more typical, is the first marriage of the main female character. That marriage began for her as an escape from her family, and it is disastrous. Her first husband is much like Ellen's father, and his abuse of her ends with his early death. Her second, and happy marriage, perhaps seems less unequal to her because her second husband, although poor like her first, is so far superior as a human being to her first.

Later novels illustrate other sorts of inequalities or marked differences between the marriage partners. In both of the family sagas, unsuccessful marriages of various sorts are depicted. In these cases, the males are generally shown to be less sensitive than their wives, sometimes overly materialistic or simply weak, but generally unworthy of them. These characterizations, with the added example of Ellen's father in *Ellen Foster*, have led to some objections to Gibbons's characterizations of men. As noted earlier, however, these two novels have for their subjects matriarchal families, so Gibbons necessarily had to remove the men from her story lines or subordinate them in order to maintain her focus on the women. It is also worth pointing out that at the end of the more recent of these books, *Charms for the Easy Life*, a successful marriage between equals in intellect, status, and character seems forecast for the youngest woman.

The inequalities in the remaining two books are of quite different sorts. In *Sights Unseen*, a woman with a severe mental illness is married to a middle-class man, the son of a prominent local family, and it is her incapacity which keeps her from functioning as a normal wife and mother and creates the differences between them. In *On the Occasion of My Last Afternoon*, the protagonist, a young Southern woman from a family of the aristocratic plantation class (although only newly so, and her father does not really fit in with other members of that caste) marries a Northerner. The inequality is that of political and regional background. However, in most really meaningful ways, this husband and wife are truly equals, for her childhood and youth had taught her to oppose slavery and other aspects of her culture, and she is attracted to her husband partly because he represents those values she has intentionally adopted. Another marriage, less foregrounded in the novel, is more similar to that in *Ellen Foster*. That is the marriage between the protagonist's parents. He is a man from an almost unspeakably horrible background who has achieved wealth, partly by unscrupulous means, and who finds a bride from an aristocratic but newly impoverished family whom he marries in order to gain social status. She "marries down" in status but "up" in wealth. Even more than Ellen's father, he is abusive, violent, and a racist, and like Ellen's mother, his wife is sensitive, gentle, kindly, and long-suffering. This marriage, however, endures until the wife's death from natural causes, but while it exists, the wife takes refuge in the few ways she can—in prolonged visits to neighboring plantations and in migraine headaches. The marriage itself is just as unequal and unhappy as that of Ellen Foster's parents.

Outsider Moving Toward Belonging

This plot motif, like that of unequal marriages, is treated with some variety in the novels but is somewhat less persistent. In *Ellen Foster*, it might be seen as central to the story. Ellen is an outsider in that her immediate family consists only of a father who hates and abuses her while her extended family includes a grandmother, several aunts, and a cousin, who reject and neglect her. She has no real place in her community, her only friends being the members of a black family to whom she has been taught to feel superior because of her white race, but she seeks and finally finds acceptance, first—briefly—with a teacher and then more permanently with her foster family. The device is more noticeable and important in this first novel than in the ones which follow, but it can nevertheless be detected in a number of them.

A Virtuous Woman fits less easily into this category, except that the wife's history can be interpreted as, first, an escape from a family in which she does not wish to belong, an unhappy first marriage in which she is reduced to poverty and menial work, and then a happy and fulfilling second marriage. Her first marriage brings no sense of community, but the second one does.

In *Charms for the Easy Life*, Charlie Kate, the grandmother, moves literally from the country to the city, but more important, she moves from being an uneducated folk healer and midwife to being a respected member of a civic and a medical community. She achieves her belonging by her dedication and hard work and by her care for those less able to care for themselves. In *Sights Unseen*, the movement is quite different. Here a woman, severely mentally ill, is returned to sanity and enabled to participate in the life of her family. And in *On the Occasion of My Last Afternoon*, the protagonist moves from a family in which she always feels an outsider, because of her antislavery beliefs and her love of learning, to a marriage in which she is an equal to a husband who shares and works for the same things she values.

Strong Black Female Characters

In several of the novels, a strong black woman plays an important role, twice serving as a surrogate mother for a central character. In *Ellen Foster*, this motif is passed over relatively quickly, but it is nevertheless significant. A field hand looks after and helps Ellen when her grandmother puts her to brutal physical labor for which she is completely unprepared. Without Mavis's help and support, Ellen would have been hard put to endure this trial, and she comes to admire Mavis, even to the point of secretly spying on her family and constructing daydreams about them. For a brief time during some of her worst days, Mavis enables Ellen to survive.

More important are strong black women in Gibbons's latest two novels, both of who support and nurture characters who are greatly in need of help. In *Sights Unseen*, Pearl is housekeeper, cook, and general maid for the family, but more important, she is the center, the one who keeps the family able to function and the one who rears the children. It is the kitchen over which she presides where they find refuge, where they do their homework, and where they have a sense of family. It is she who attempts to help them understand their mother's illness and who cares for the mother during her worst times of incapacitation.

Similarly, in *On the Occasion of My Last Afternoon*, Clarice is officially a cook and housekeeper but fulfills many more functions. She had rescued the protagonist's father from his unspeakable childhood and had tried, but failed, to rear him into a responsible adult. She remains with the family, partly because of her regret at how he had turned out, and she is as much a mother to his children as is their own gentle but ineffectual mother. When the protagonist marries, Pearl accompanies her to her new home, and there she teaches her about running a household and about caring for her husband and children. In some senses she serves as a kind of moral compass for the protagonist's family.

Pearl and Clarice, as is observed elsewhere, are similar to a number of other strong black women in Southern fiction. Harper Lee's Calpurnia of *To Kill a Mockingbird* and Carson McCullers's Berenice in *The Member of the Wedding* come to mind. A somewhat earlier example is William Faulkner's Dilsey in *The Sound and the Fury*. All these are presented as admirable characters, as personages not only of strength and dignity but also as individuals who are absolutely essential to the functioning of the families they serve. That there are difficulties with this character type may be seen by adding one additional example, that of Mammy in Margaret Mitchell's *Gone with the Wind*. These strong black women, no matter how admirable, represent a stereotype. Gibbons's examples of this stereotyped character, however, are at least notable for the individuality which she gives them. They have flaws and weaknesses, and so become rounded depictions. Clarice, particularly, because of one action, that is, her concealment of the freed status of three other servants, as well as her lasting sense of guilt for the deception, is more fully realized and human than her origins in a stereotype might lead a critic to expect.

Tyrannical Father Figures

Although the repeating strong black female figure is a benevolent character, another repeating character, a strong white male, is anything but kindly. This character is a father or grandfather who tyrannizes over his family, particularly the protagonist daughter or granddaughter, controlling and overwhelming her. Such figures appears in three of the novels and are among Gibbons's more memorable characters.

In *Ellen Foster*, Ellen's father, an alcoholic and a resentful and angry man who abuses both his sensitive wife and his daughter, represents this type. Spunky and resourceful, Ellen resists, mostly passively, his ill-treatment until he attempts to abuse her sexually and then she escapes his domination with relief. Emma Garnet's father in *On the Occasion of My Last Afternoon* is similar in many ways, despite living over a hundred years earlier. Like Ellen's father, Mr. Tate is tyrannical and abusive, caring for no one except himself. Like the earlier character, he has come from an impoverished childhood, and he was also horribly abused psychologically. Like Ellen, Emma Garnet is a strong young character and manages to escape from his attempts at controlling her life. Her methods of escape are different, but they are similarly motivated. What is most different, however, about the depiction given the two characters is that Mr. Tate is more fully characterized, and explanations are given for his character flaws and behavior.

The third example of this character type occurs in *Sights Unseen* and compared with the others is a relatively benign figure. A true patriarch, Hattie's grandfather is a little less controlling than the others, a little less demanding that his wishes be instantly obeyed, and a little less certain of his right to exercise absolute power over his family. The difference is that he does concern himself about the welfare of his relatives. He is particularly concerned about his mentally ill daughter-in-law, for whom he feels a deep affection, and he tends to sacrifice the welfare of others to what he perceives as her needs, but at least, unlike the others, his motivations may be seen as relatively compassionate.

Mother-Daughter Relationships

All of Gibbons's novels are rich in relationships, and some are centered on the relationships between mothers and daughters. *Ellen Foster* portrays a daughter who tragically loses her mother and spends the rest of the book seeking a replacement. *A Virtuous Woman* shows a woman who yearns for but never achieves children of her own, and so she finds an outlet for her maternal longings by becoming a kind of unofficial foster mother for the neglected daughter of a neighbor. *A Cure for Dreams* and *Charms for the Easy Life* follow several generations of mothers and daughters, showing most of these relationships to be emotionally rich. *Sights*

Unseen centers around a mother incapacitated by mental illness and her young daughter who struggles to understand. And *On the Occasion of My Last Afternoon*, which fits less easily into this particular pattern, depicts a daughter who loves her mother deeply but fails to rescue her from her unhappy situation and who then, with the assistance of her black surrogate mother, successfully rears three daughters of her own.

3

Ellen Foster
(1987)

Gibbons's first and most directly autobiographical novel, *Ellen Foster*, remains her most widely read and admired. Suitable for young adults yet appealing to mature readers, it quickly reached a wide audience, somewhat unusual for a first novel, and it has retained its popularity. The young writer gave to her protagonist a number of her own characteristics and experiences, but her active imagination (similar to Ellen's) enabled her to go beyond her own life story and create a character who truly comes alive on the page, about whom readers not only empathize with but also who they both like and admire for her courage in the face of terrible troubles.

The novel is the story of a young girl whose immediate family is destroyed and whose extended family does not care about her but who manages, by her own spunk, intelligence, and determination, to find a new and happier situation. The title is taken from the full name, which, at the end of the book, stands for her new identity. The book takes as its basic premises the situation and character of the title character, and it studies what happens when a woman from the Southern middle class "marries down," that is, marries a man below her in status. The disastrous marriage of Ellen's mother and father is what sets the action of the novel into motion.

PLOT DEVELOPMENT, STRUCTURE, AND
NARRATIVE METHOD

Ellen Foster is very simple in plot and yet complex in narrative method and structure. The story line covers just over a year in the life of a young girl from an extremely dysfunctional family as she lives through the tragic death of her beloved mother, and seeks to escape her abusive father and find a real home and family. The novel's plot, therefore, can be quickly summed up by a simple listing of her living situations: with both parents, with her father after her mother's death, briefly with her friend Starletta's family, and then with her Aunt Betsy after fleeing her abusive father, with her father again after the aunt rejects her, with her teacher Julia and Julia's husband Roy, with her maternal grandmother after court intervention to return her to her natural family, with her Aunt Nadine and cousin Dora after the grandmother's death, and finally (and happily) with a new foster family. The events of the novel, a nearly unbroken series of deaths and rejections, are punctuated by episodes in which Ellen finds some love and support, principally from Starletta and her parents and from Julia and Roy. These few supports are for a long time overbalanced by the physical abuse from her father and the emotional abuse of every person related to her by blood except her mother.

But the texture of the novel is more complicated than this summary suggests. First there is the character of Ellen herself, to be discussed more fully below. Here it is enough to suggest that her courage and insistence on her worth, as well as her sometimes funny and often imaginative methods of coping with her terrible situation, indicate that she is a survivor and make the tone of the novel actually quite hopeful.

The novel's narrative method also adds complexity to what might have been a very simple, almost naïve tale. Gibbons has made use of a tightly restricted point of view—Ellen tells her own story herself, in her own way, using her own language, and frankly revealing her actions and feelings. But she does not follow a chronological time sequence. Instead, she shifts back and forth between her past and her present, by implication separating her life into two major periods: A terrible past in which she was repeatedly victimized but refused to consider herself a victim and a wonderful present in which she has everything she needs to make her happy.

The novel opens, for example, in the past and establishes from the very first line that Ellen's family life is unhappy: "When I was little I would think of ways to kill my daddy" (1). That this is not the typical anger of a rebellious child angered at ordinary discipline is quickly revealed by her comments on her daddy's drunkenness. And by the second page, Ellen's narrative shows that her life is now much better: "I live in a clean brick house and mostly I am left to myself" (2); she sums up her experience by saying, "I figure I made out pretty good considering the rest of my family is either dead or crazy" (2). From the very beginning of the book, then, readers know that everything will turn out well and that the story will reveal how Ellen got from her painful beginnings to her happy ending. By having the narrative move back and forth between the past and the present, Gibbons skillfully and repeatedly reminds readers of the contrast between Ellen's two lives and the fact that she will ultimately prevail. At first glance, it may seem that Ellen tells her story in a disjointed way, not being able to follow the thread of events as they happened, but this is not an accurate description of the way the narrative works. While the happy present is in general shown as an undifferentiated, almost static life in which nothing changes—in which she has enough to eat, a clean room to live in, a pony to ride, and a mama to love her—the events of the past are narrated in chronological order. The present is a goal that she has reached, but the past was a series of experiences she lived through. And this interpretation of her life experience is emphasized by the shifting between past and present.

CHARACTER DEVELOPMENT

Ellen Foster is tightly constructed around its central character: Ellen is both the protagonist and the narrator, and her experiences and perspective on what happens to her make up the material of the book. Through most of her narrative, Ellen does not see other characters as individuals in their own rights (although this is changing in the novel's last pages) but only as they impinge on her own life. Some characters could be interpreted as caricatures (figures who are depicted through one characteristic which is exaggerated rather than being fully developed), but what is crucial for the novel is not what they are really like as human beings but how they affect Ellen and how they appear to this eleven-year-old girl.

Ellen is bright, sometimes understanding people and events with a perception lacking in people much older than herself, but she is also naïve, sometimes misunderstanding simple facts of her society and culture. She can understand the pathos of her mother's life and her grandmother's resulting anger, but she errs in so simple a matter as confusing the name "Foster" with the common adjective used to describe a family which takes in children who have become wards of society. These characteristics, along with her sometimes childish language and attitudes, make her a believable young girl—she is ten years old when the novel opens and lives through her eleventh birthday and two Christmases during the course of the book.

Ellen is a stubbornly determined young person, one who seems secure in her sense of self-worth. Indeed, the racism with which she struggles through her story may be seen as a way of propping up her belief in her own value. Coming from living conditions that would only identify her as "poor white trash" and living with a shiftless drunk of a father, she can claim to be better than few people. But black people in her society, even if responsible and sober citizens, automatically occupy the lowest social class, and thus someone like Ellen can find comfort in being better than they are.

Particularly revealing of her personality are her symbols or images, those things which represent to her the difference between her life during the main action of the novel and her goals. Perhaps appropriately for a very young person, those images are very concrete. She often mentions types of houses, food, and clothing (Groover has discussed the latter two at some length in a helpful comparison of the novel with Mark Twain's *The Adventures of Huckleberry Finn*). Particularly telling is the mention of all three of these things in the novel's opening, as she first sets up her hatred of her father when he was alive and how much better off she is in her present. She does not describe her early house, food, or clothing, but by the implications of context, they are far inferior to the "clean brick house" she now lives in, the food that is immediately replaced by a trip to the grocery store when needed, and her "stylish well-groomed self" who now waits for the school bus (2). Throughout the novel she frequently describes physical objects—the decorations which she is not supposed to touch, for example, in her grandmother's and aunts' houses and which clearly to her represent both the material comfort she yearns for and her relatives' emotional repression and their rejection of her. But she is not really materialistic in the sense that she does not want things just for the sake of having them. This is indicated by her scorn of her relatives' useless decorative possessions and by her odd method of dressing and shopping for clothes. She buys duplicate garments which are a size larger than she is currently wearing, so as to save the trouble of having to make daily decisions on her clothing (113). Even the game she invents in the bad times at her father's house is based on physical objects of daily life. She calls her game "catalog." It consists of picking out for an imagined family of "mom, the dad, the cute children" all sorts of items, from kitchen to camping equipment (31).

Ellen is a surprisingly bookish girl for one with so little encouragement in that direction. She is an ambitious reader and is up to the Brontes on a list a teacher has compiled for her; she also mentions her pleasure in Chaucer's "Wife of Bath's Tale" (11). The regular arrival of the book-mobile is an important event in her life (40), and a prized possession in her original home is a set of encyclopedias. She loves to browse in them, and even though she is not certain they really belong to her (they had probably been owned by her mother), she believes that much reading in them has made them hers. After her father's death, her hate-filled grand-mother burns both the flag representing his military service and the en-cyclopedias; Ellen says the flag is not important but she resents the destruction of the encyclopedias (40, 83).

If Ellen is not materialistic in the usual sense, she nevertheless is al-ways very aware of things. She is equally aware of people's relationships with her, and these relationships are often emphasized by her use of the possessive pronoun "my" in connection with people. She identifies most of the other characters by their relationship with her, not by their actual names; indeed readers never learn the names of many characters and are in fact never given the true last name of any character. Some impor-tant family members are referred to always as "my mama," "my daddy," "my mama's mama." Among her relatives only her aunts Betsy and Na-dine and cousin Dora have names, perhaps indicating their particularly great distance from her. Indeed she does seem to describe them with particularly great detachment. Additionally, there is "my new mama" and sometimes even "my Starletta." In the reference to Starletta, "my" seems to carry overtones of affection, but most often her uses of the possessive pronoun emphasize the importance of the individual, for good or for bad, in Ellen's life.

All other characters are seen through the lens of Ellen's personality and situation, so they are not nearly as fully rounded as she is. They are important not for what they are in themselves but for how they affect the book's protagonist. As a result there are elements of stereotype in many of them, and many seem exaggerated, not quite believable. That they are not fully rounded is not really important, however, for what

matters is how Ellen sees them and how they impact on her life. As a
result our discussion of these characters also often becomes a discussion
of Ellen, too.

Of great importance, although seen briefly, is Ellen's mother, always
referred to as "my mama." Why she married Ellen's father is a mystery,
one which Ellen never puzzles over but which readers must simply accept. The two parents are totally mismatched and miserable with each
other. To begin with, Ellen's mother had "married down," having come
from a much higher social class than her father. The marriage had been
opposed, quite rightly it seems, by her family, which had essentially cast
her off as a result of it. This explains the lack of contact between Ellen
and her mother's family, as well as her grandmother's resentment, even
hatred, of her. "My mama," as Ellen calls her, was a gentle and loving
woman, and Ellen recalls with pleasure the brief period when her mother
was healthy enough to work in her garden. Ellen, too young to be very
much help, picked up the little piles of weeds. But the mother is sickly,
often ill, and her death, an intentional overdose of her heart medication,
is precipitated by her cruel and selfish treatment by her husband when
she returns home from a stay in the hospital. Her shiftless and cruel
husband has broken her, and even her love for Ellen is not enough to
inspire her to cling to life. Ellen tries to protect her mother from her
father's abuse, and then she lies beside her as she dies. The depth of
Ellen's love for her mother is touchingly revealed by her brief comment:
"You can rest with me until somebody comes to get you" (12).

It is the death of this "sweet woman" that causes Ellen's quest. No
matter how horrible Ellen's father made their home, so long as her
mother was there, Ellen had security and love. After her death, Ellen
looks back to their brief times together as a kind of golden past that she
strives to recapture with a new mother and home. For a time, she always
wears some item of her mother's clothing (27–28), a way of keeping her
with her, and she chooses her "new mama" as the person most possible
to "make into a new mama" (68). Her birth mother, no matter how weak,
ineffectual, sad, and defeated, gives to Ellen an ideal, someone with
whom to compare possible substitute mothers.

Ellen's father, whose given name is "Bill" (13, 43), but whom she always calls simply "my daddy," is presented as a brutal tyrant. He is an
unpleasant drunk, who brings his drinking buddies to the house; who
domineers over his sick wife, insisting that she serve his trivial wants
when she is just home from the hospital; who beats her but is careful
not to leave any marks; and who finally attempts to rape Ellen. He hates

his gentle wife, or so Ellen believes (5), and he takes out his hatred of his wife on his daughter. The only possible good thing readers ever learn of him is that he is a veteran of military service, when, after his death and funeral, which Ellen and her grandmother do not attend, his brother brings Ellen a flag folded in a triangle (81). Perhaps, had Ellen been more curious, she might have discovered experiences in his military service which would explain his deterioration into the destroyed and destructive man the novel presents. But coming to an understanding of his past is not of interest to Ellen—or to readers—and no additional hints are given. His function in the story is to serve as a villain, and that is how Ellen sees him.

Like "my daddy," "my mama's mama" is presented as almost purely evil. But Ellen understands her anger and hatred for herself and her father as misplaced love for her daughter (Ellen's mother) and resentment at how that gentle soul had been destroyed by her unfortunate marriage to Ellen's father. The grandmother had cut the mother off when she "married down" in social class. To the grandmother, with her firmly held convictions about the separation of social classes and races, marrying her daughter was the father's first great sin, and his drinking and abuse of his wife apparently seem related to his lower-class origins. The grandmother ignores Ellen until her daughter's funeral, and during that occasion she has as little as possible to do with her grandchild. She makes no attempt to remove Ellen from what is clearly a terrible home situation until much later, after the child has already been removed from her home and her father has made an issue of her removal by coming, drunk, to her school and creating a scene. Only then, perhaps because of her shame at having her granddaughter's situation become very public, does the grandmother go to court to have Ellen given into her own custody. The ironic result is that Ellen is removed not from her abusive father but from a temporary home in which she is cherished and where she is happy.

When Ellen comes into the grandmother's home, she is once again ignored and then is sent to work in the fields, doing physically difficult stoop labor in the hot sun. Her grandmother wants to teach her a lesson, she says, to crush from her any resemblance to her father. Her physical abuse of Ellen is indirect, for she never lays a hand on her, but she causes her as much pain as her father ever had. Ellen recognizes that her grandmother's behavior is not rational, but wishes she could discover the exact name and nature of her ailment, and then realizes she can't. "What would you look under? Meanness? Anger? Just crazy?" (77). She does come to understand that in her grandmother's twisted way of thinking, she is herself "a substitute for my daddy" (79). And then when her grandmother becomes ill, ironically the grandmother makes her into a substitute for her mother, expecting Ellen to care for her. And Ellen does care for her, with as much determination as she had cared for the mother she so dearly loved. It is during this period of the grandmother's illness that Ellen pieces together her story. She does not describe her detective work, although a number of clues have been given in the earlier narrative. She learns that the grandmother had first spied on her daughter's family and then obtained legal possession of Ellen's father's land, doling out an allowance to him—an allowance on which he and Ellen had lived and which had supplied him with his drinking money. The grandmother's anger and resentment had led her to spy on and take control of her daughter's family's lives even while holding herself aloof from them both publicly and privately. Her death, coming quite soon after that of her despised son-in-law, suggests that she had so allowed her anger to possess her that when its principal target is dead she can survive no longer. Eaten up by hatred, she has nothing else to live for—but, controlling to the end, she demands that Ellen care for her.

The rest of Ellen's family, all female, are the grandmother's creatures. There seems little difference between the two aunts, Betsy and Nadine, except that Ellen seeks help first from Betsy and that Nadine has a daughter, Dora. Betsy is perhaps a bit more hypocritical than Nadine, for she acts as if she is delighted to take Ellen in, if only for a weekend, and to pamper her for that brief time. Nadine, who receives custody of Ellen after the grandmother's death, makes it clear immediately that she is taking in her niece only out of duty, and Ellen receives no pampering in her household, always being ostentatiously treated as inferior to Dora. Ellen does not refer to any of these three with her usual possessive pronoun; it is always "Betsy" or "Nadine" or "Dora," never "my aunt" or "my Dora." She feels no pull from their ties of kinship, nor any emotional attachment, as with "my Starletta."

The rest of the novel's characters lack any blood relationship with Ellen. They represent the various ways the outside world—friends, school, court system—affect Ellen. In Starletta and her parents and in Julia and Roy, Ellen finds loving and supportive families who treat her kindly. Starletta's parents, despite their deep poverty, take her in as one of their own despite the racial difference of which Ellen is deeply aware. When she is cold, Starletta's father buys her a coat that is every bit as good as the one he buys his own daughter. When her own family—

father, grandmother, and aunts—ignore her at Christmas, Starletta's mother makes her a sweater, causing Ellen to cry, an unusual display of emotion for her. Consisting of mother, father, and daughter just like Ellen's original family, they model the love, caring, and kindness so rare in Ellen's experience, and, although she does not know it for a long time, they give her an example of what she is searching for.

Starletta herself is important both as Ellen's only real friend and as an important figure in Gibbons's development of the theme of race. Ellen sees Starletta as a follower, someone she can lead, and also as an inferior. When she first appears, at the funeral of Ellen's mother, Ellen's mixed feelings about her are immediately clear. She both wishes she can sit with Starletta's family instead of with her own and emphasizes Starletta's inferiority to her by saying that she and her mother "both eat dirt" but that her own father had punished her for doing the same thing. She comments honestly throughout the novel on the separation she wants to maintain from Starletta because of Starletta's race. And at the end of the novel, her growth in maturity is shown through her intentional rejection of the racism that had been an important part of her self-image. Starletta remains a somewhat shadowy figure, not seen directly very often, more present in Ellen's thoughts than in the action of the novel. She says little, and several critics and reviewers have erroneously described her as mute. However, it is revealed at the end of the novel that she stutters and becomes frustrated when she sometimes has difficulty getting her words out (145). Interestingly, Ellen does not comment on this problem of Starletta's earlier in the novel when she might have used it as another indication of Starletta's inferiority. Instead, she withholds her mention of this detail until the point at which she has overcome her racist ideas and finally can be completely sympathetic of the handicaps under which Starletta and her family live.

Relatively minor in importance in the novel, but paralleling Starletta's family and thus reemphasizing their functions, are Mavis and her family. Mavis is the black woman who takes Ellen under her wing when Ellen is set to work in the fields. Her kindness is the only good aspect of life at her grandmother's home. Mavis teaches her how to do the work and tries to make it as easy for her as possible. In the evenings, Ellen flees her grandmother's comfortable home to go down the path toward Mavis's cabin so she can watch Mavis's happy family life, so different from what she is experiencing with her grandmother—so different, in fact, from anything she has ever experienced except with Starletta's family and with Julia and Roy.

Julia and Roy, Ellen's art teacher and her husband, provide for Ellen the one period of happiness and security during the body of the novel. They take her in without hesitation when signs of her father's physical abuse are observed at her school. They are just as different from her as are Starletta and her family, but their difference is not in race. Rather it is in background and lifestyle. They have come from the North and are not really part of the culture of this unnamed community. They are, Ellen says, former flower children from the sixties. When Ellen, aware of how little they fit in, asks where they have come from, Julia, equally aware of being an outsider, initially says, "Pluto" (57). Their differentness is indicated by the facts that Julia is an art teacher, the professional in the family, and Roy stays home to tend the house and garden. They are free from the prejudices and inhibitions of the small Southern town where they have somehow come to live.

Their love for Ellen is warm and nurturing, the only thing that really matters to her or to them. When Ellen's grandmother sues for custody, Julia buys a dress for Ellen to wear to court which both Julia and Ellen hate. Playing the game, however, is not enough. The judge, in a hearing that Ellen considers a sham, gives custody to the grandmother. Roy and Julia drop out of the narrative after this point, except that Ellen mentions later that Julia has been fired from her local teaching job, so they have left the community, and that Julia writes to her from time to time (71). Julia's unconventionality probably explains why a local school board would fire her, and her continuing love and concern for Ellen are revealed by her letters.

Three other characters, none of whom is given either a name or a label with "my," represent aspects of the social structure which affect Ellen in some way. All are basically kindly in intent, but none is of any assistance to her. They are men who wish her well but who have no understanding of her or her situation. All three make only brief appearances in the text and none is of particular importance to her, yet each is sharply characterized in his brief appearance.

The first of these is the undertaker who officiates at the funeral of Ellen's mother. She always refers to him as "the smiling man," capturing in this phrase the unctuous quality of the stereotypical funeral director, who must live his days earning his living from the grief of the recently bereaved, as Ellen understands. But his professional insincerity seems not really to bother her, and she describes with little comment his activities as he shepherds the family through the funeral activities.

More important are the other two representatives of society, because they are assigned functions which do matter in Ellen's life. The judge who decides on her custody and the school counselor who tries to care for her emotional well-being after she comes into the child protective system both want to do what is best for her, but neither is able to see her and her birth family as they really are. Both of these functionaries do their best for her, but each is blinded by the accepted beliefs of his time and profession, so that he is unable to understand Ellen or be of any help to her. The judge is sure that birth families should be kept together whenever possible and does not even try to investigate Ellen's actual family. In fact, he never asks her what she would prefer or what her family is like. He simply assumes, probably because Ellen's grandmother has requested custody, that keeping Ellen with the grandmother is best (66).

The school counselor administers Rorschach psychological tests (the ink blots that Ellen mocks as "pictures of flat bats" [2]), as he tries to discover how badly damaged emotionally she has been by her experiences, and he finds deep psychological meaning in things that Ellen explains to herself much more simply. When she begins signing her name "Ellen Foster," taking on the last name she mistakenly believes belongs to her "new mama," he sees her change in last name as an indication she is suffering from an identity problem. Ellen listens to him—after all, as she recognizes, he is "paid good money . . . to find whatever ails me and cure it" (101). He does not listen to her explanation of what her adoption of the new name means, and so she finally decides she will not be seeing him again. This declaration is a kind of statement of independence, of rejection of the attempts of the social and legal system to do for her what she can do better for herself. At the end of the novel, she acknowledges that she does have some adjustment problems, but with the help of her new mother and with her own good common sense and self-awareness she is working on them, and willpower and trust are part of this. Ellen is a survivor, and with her own hard work, despite the interference in her life of judges and school counselors, she is coming through all the horrors of her young life.

The last character of importance, referred to throughout the novel as "my new mama," is the one who enables Ellen to have her happy ending. Ellen never gives any direct description of her, and readers' understanding of her comes gradually, as more and more bits of information are given. We learn first that Ellen, in her happy present, lives in a nice house and is well fed and groomed (2), but piece by piece we learn more about life there and about the woman who makes this life possible. She is a single woman who cares for a number of foster children, partly assisted by her church. Although the children all seem to have special problems of their own (one, for example, is a teenage mother with her baby), "my new mama" always seems to have time for Ellen and to understand what she needs. Like the judge and the school counselor, she has an official connection to the child protective system, for otherwise she could not have arranged for Ellen to come to stay with her when she flees the aunt to whom the judge had given custody. She says there will not be a problem about Ellen's staying with her, and it happens as she has said. Unlike the judge and counselor, however, she sees Ellen as she is, listens to what Ellen says about herself and her experiences, and understands what Ellen needs. With her, Ellen finds a resting place where all the material things she needs, such as food and clothes, are provided. But more important, she finds love, stability, and a place where she can begin to heal emotionally.

SETTING

In one sense, setting is basic to *Ellen Foster*, but in another sense it seems almost unimportant. Characters, society, and plot assume the placing of the novel in the American southeast, presumably Gibbons's own North Carolina, but that locale is only rarely described or directly emphasized. Attitudes about race and class basic to the novel and characteristic of the South underlie its action, so that the novel cannot be understood without reference to its Southern setting. But because it is the only place Ellen knows, she does not comment on the "Southernness" of the things she describes. Her small town, her awareness of the division between black and white people, her knowledge of the emphasis on social caste—all these things, typical of the rural South she knows, are simply the way the world is, to her, and therefore are not worth special comment. Thus, readers never learn precisely where the story takes place. Neither the town nor the state are ever named. Only as they are relevant are some descriptions given: of the drive through the town on the way to her father's funeral (21), for example. Descriptions of interiors, for instance those of the houses in which her female relatives live, are the fullest and most specific, as Ellen sharply observes the objects that are important to these women, indirectly commenting on their materialism, as well as her own lack of experience with middle-class life.

The time in which the actions of the novel occur is also assumed rather than specified. For example, there are allusions to the flower child past of Julia and Roy, which Ellen places in the 1960s (57). The symbolic use of the folded flag in connection with Ellen's father, indicating past military service, might imply that his drinking and cruelty were caused by the horrors of service in Vietnam, experiences which did in fact cause horrible psychological problems to many veterans. However, such suggestions are never in any way stated. They do, however, increase the probability that the novel takes place some time after the Vietnam War, and thus they also indicate a time period some time after the late 1970s.

THEMES

Several central themes—family, search for identity, and race—control Ellen's narration of her experience. The first, family—or, more precisely, her search for a mother and family—is the central focus of the plot, while the second, race, is examined and eventually resolved through the search for the first. Critic Kristina K. Groover (1999) has pointed out that Gibbons's depiction of Ellen's life is an example of the very old quest motif (found as far back as Homer's *Odyssey*), only altered in profound ways. In her comparison and contrast of *Ellen Foster* with *The Adventures of Huckleberry Finn*, a great masterpiece of American literature, Groover comments that the two novels are similar in a number of ways—the youth of their protagonists, their abusive and alcoholic fathers, their Southern backgrounds, their struggles with racism despite having an interracial friendship, and their persistent journey toward their goals. But as she indicates, the differences between the two novels are also very important. Perhaps most basic, Ellen is female, and her quest is from its outset very different from Huck's male journey. Where he literally travels over a relatively large geographic area and ends his quest by beginning a new one (his decision to head west), she simply moves from household to household, always remaining in or near the same small town. More crucially, while Huck's goal is freedom from civilization and domesticity for himself and from slavery for his black friend Jim, Ellen's goal is to find herself a place in civilization, a home, and a mother. He tries to escape from all family ties, whether of blood or not, but she must escape her ties of blood in order to find a real family and nurturance.

The families involved in Ellen's journey can be classified in several ways: as related by blood or unrelated, as nurturing or as illustrating several sorts of abuse, as black or white, as middle-class or lower class.

Those related to her by blood, with the single exception of the mother whose death sets off Ellen's journey, are abusive, either physically like her father or emotionally like her aunt Betsy (who almost gaily rejects her) and her aunt Nadine (who pampers her own spoiled daughter while treating Ellen like an ungrateful and unwanted interloper). Her grandmother is both emotionally and physically abusive. She ignores Ellen, berating her for being her father's daughter, maintaining total emotional distance from the girl. Eventually she goes so far as to have Ellen put to work in the hot fields, doing labor that is hard for the field hands she also exploits. The grandmother's physical abuse is perhaps indirect, as she never touches the child, but that does not lessen its effect.

The nurturing families, all unrelated to Ellen, are quite varied. Starletta and her parents are black and poor. Julia and Roy are defined as middle class by her profession as a teacher but are unconventional, as described by Ellen, "flower children" who are still living in the 1960s (57). They take Ellen into their home although they have no obligation to do so, and it seems clear that they would have been delighted to adopt her if the court would have allowed it. The few months she spends with them are a brief but happy time for her. A minor character, Mavis, one of the black field hands with whom Ellen works, takes her under her protection and teaches her something about what family can be as Ellen "spies on" her family in the evenings. And finally and most important, there is the foster mother and her other foster children with whom Ellen finally reaches emotional and physical security.

The one other family of importance to the novel consists of Starletta and her parents. They are also central to the theme of race, which is less a structural element than the theme of family, but its development is of equal importance to the novel. Indeed, the theme of family can be seen as relating to how Ellen lives while the theme of race relates to who she is—and to how she changes during the course of the novel. It is closely bound to her sense of identity, and it reveals her growth in maturity throughout her experience. Tracing her comments on race, particularly on how she sees her place in society as compared with that of the African Americans she knows, shows how she grows in understanding of both herself and others.

Particularly revealing and combining the themes of family and race are Ellen's comments on Starletta and her parents. Ellen's first mention of Starletta, seeing her and her parents at the funeral of Ellen's father, reveals immediately how mixed her feelings are. She notices and comments on Starletta's cleanliness, as if she were surprised by it, but she adds that she wishes she could sit with her and her parents. Comments follow on how Starletta and her mother eat dirt and that her own father has punished her for doing the same thing. Starletta and her family are somehow representative of that which is good and that which must be avoided. Only somewhat later, however, when she indicates that Starletta's family does its shopping in "colored town" (they are, in fact, buying a winter coat for Ellen, something her own family does not provide and something they surely cannot afford [30]) is it revealed that this family is in fact African American. That fact, however, becomes very important in Ellen's relationship with her friend and her friend's family.

Starletta's family always treats Ellen with warmth and is nurturing of her. But Ellen regularly reminds herself, and her readers, of the gulf that is between them because of the racial difference. She both respects them and looks down on them. She is scornful of the constant smell of food and cooking in their house and their lack of indoor plumbing (35–36), but she respects the fact that they "do not try to be white" (35). Most significantly, she sees contact with them as somehow polluting. She thinks she could not drink after them (35), and she is troubled at eating in their house. But these deep and irrational fears of contamination by her friend's family are occasionally lessened, and she readily accepts their kindnesses. She accepts the coat Starletta's father buys for her, and when Starletta's mother gives her a sweater for Christmas, she specifically says, "it does not look colored at all" (38). When she flees for safety to Starletta's home, she sleeps in the same bed with Starletta's mother but maintains her separateness by wearing her coat and not getting under the covers (47). The love of these kind people is able to weaken the racial prejudices she has been taught by her own family and by society but she stubbornly holds on to them nevertheless.

Ellen's awareness of racial distinctions remains a problem, however, through much of the book. When Julia and Roy ask her whom she would like to invite to her birthday party, the only person she can think of is Starletta, who remains her only real friend despite their difference in race. That she understands the rules of her segregated society is made clear when she describes their trip to the movies where "Starletta was the only colored girl at the movies" (60). She knows the rules but is willing to break them.

Without any hesitation, Roy and Julia entertain Starletta at Ellen's birthday celebration, in contrast to the racist behavior and language throughout of Ellen's own family. Her gradual awakening to the irrationality of racism accompanies her increasing understanding of her family's shallowness and rejection of her. Others, both black and white, who are good to her—Starletta and her family, Mavis, Roy and Julia, her "new mama"—reject racial distinctions as meaningless and give her good models of understanding and acceptance.

All this is revealed in the later pages of the book. A meditation on race and her own growth in understanding (99–100) is placed next to two contrasting pieces of material: her life with her grandmother in the past and her frustration with the school counselor who over-intellectualizes (so she thinks) her changing sense of her own identity. In that meditation, Ellen reveals that she now sees Starletta as an individual who is complete in herself, with her own feelings and ideas, not as someone who is useful in making her own life more pleasant. "You can never be sure about how somebody else thinks about you except if they beat it into your head," she says (99), suggesting a truly felt realization that Starletta does in fact have her own ideas, feelings, and life, something she had not consciously known previously. And she specifically connects that realization with her desire to invite Starletta to her home, although she hesitates, still because of the racial division. Nevertheless, she now realizes how much she has changed and how she has lost some of her racist attitudes. She is ashamed that among her former requirements for a new family were that it be white and have running water (100). And she is sure that her new mother will allow her to invite Starletta to their home, one sign of her trust in her new mother.

Immediately after this discussion, Ellen shifts to the session in which the counselor had tried, by remarking on her having adopted a new last name, "Foster," to force her to examine what he sees as her confused sense of identity. It turns out that she has intended to adopt her new mother's last name, having been misled when told earlier that she and the children with her were a "foster family" (103). Her use of the new name, in her view, is an indication of her certainty of identity, not of any confusion. She did not like the old name, and she now casts it off just as she has broken all ties with the birth family it connected her to. At the same time, she has taken what she thought was the name of her new family, thus publicly showing that they were now her chosen kinfolks. What seemed to the overintellectualizing counselor a revelation of a weak identity is to Ellen an obvious symbol of a strong, new sense of who she is and where she belongs in the world.

One final comment: When Ellen, with her new mother's happy permission, brings Starletta home for a weekend, she both repeats what she had done in having her to the birthday party at Julia and Roy's and goes far beyond what she had done then. At her teacher's home, she included Starletta because she was fond of her and because she couldn't think of anyone else to invite to a party. When she brings Starletta to her new home, she consciously intends to made amends to her friend for the racist feelings that Starletta did not know she had but which she now sees as unworthy of their friendship. She plans minutely for their activities during the weekend, all of these plans being centered around her finally apologizing to Starletta for her unfair feelings in the past. And now in an accidental but wonderful detail she demonstrates her new ability to see Starletta as an independent human being by explaining the reason Starletta had spoken little during the course of the novel—she stutters and frustration at her difficulty in speaking often keeps her silent. This detail is accidental, of course, in that Gibbons added it late to explain why Starletta's voice is little heard during the novel's action, but its placement here can be seen as one more detail revealing Ellen's growth (for another view of this last point, see Monteith's [1999] stimulating essay). And finally, not only has her old sense of being superior to at least Starletta because she was herself white been destroyed by recognition of Starletta's personhood, but also her feeling of being particularly unfortunate in her situation and proud of what she has done to overcome it has given way to an awareness that Starletta "came even farther" (146). In the moving last lines of the novel, she says, "And all this time, I thought I had the hardest row to hoe. That will always amaze me" (146)

STYLE AND IMAGERY

Ellen's story, narrated by herself, is written in her own language. Her style is naïve; sentences tend to be grammatically simple, joined by "and" or "but." The spelling is conventional, but punctuation is sparse and consists almost entirely of periods. An occasional comma appears, and question marks are used when appropriate. Ellen generally uses standard grammar, but the occasional idiomatic grammatical error appears, for example, when she says that "me and Julia and Roy worked in the garden" (58). The narrative succeeds well in conveying the flavor of the speech of a young Southerner without allowing the text to become difficult to read, as sometimes happens to narratives using unconventional spelling and more heavily colloquial or dialect-laden language. Ellen's narrative sometimes achieves a poetic quality, largely through its simplicity and concreteness of word choices and also through its occasional effective use of imagery ("spinning," to be discussed later, is the most important example).

Ellen's narrative is very specific and detailed. She is an observant young person and describes events quite precisely if sometimes in a roundabout way when she does not completely understand them or does not have the vocabulary to name them. Thus, for example, although she clearly understands the function of the undertaker, she apparently does not know a specific name for him ("undertaker," "mortician," "funeral director" might have been possibilities), and thus she always refers to him by his most obvious physical feature as "the smiling man." This technique of Gibbons's keeps Ellen's narrative voice believable and also adds vividness to the texture of the novel.

Some of the objects Ellen mentions become structurally important or symbolic. Her emphasis on food and clothing has already been mentioned. In addition, there is the microscope which she gives herself for Christmas and which she takes with her throughout her quest. When troubled or isolated, she spends her time looking through it, satisfying her curiosity about the natural world, and finding escape from her terrible experiences. Finally she uses it as a stage prop when she provokes the quarrel that causes her aunt Nadine to throw her out and enables her to reach her goal of going to her "new mama." The microscope is an obvious image for seeing, for perceiving that which most people are not aware of, and as such is an appropriate image for Ellen herself, whose ability to see and understand people and situations helps enable her to survive. For Ellen it is a toy, an escape mechanism, which she uses as she fantasizes, but it is also a scientific tool which helps her view reality. She often reminds herself that she is old Ellen not a laboratory doctor, but she longs to see actual life under the microscope and hopes to have a "professional model" some day (120–21). Always practical and realistic, Ellen finds escape in her microscope and also nourishes her active mind.

If the microscope, bought when she is very unhappy and carried with her throughout her quest, represents something of what Ellen is and her methods for surviving, a very different symbolic being, a pony, is a symbol of the relative luxury she finds in her foster mother's home. Dolphin, the pony, is mentioned from time to time, usually either in connection with her joy in riding him or her pleasure in caring for him. His presence is something very special for her in her final home.

Also noteworthy is Gibbons's use of special days to characterize the ways in which Ellen's situation changes, as well as to serve as markers of the passage of time. Two Christmases and one birthday are important days for her. The two Christmases, coming near the beginning and the end of the novel, are both unhappy times, although Ellen uses the latter as a step toward her ultimate happiness. The birthday, midway through her journey, while she is living with Julia and Roy, is a brief happy moment. Ellen reveals the emotional meaning for her of these events partly through the presents she gives and those she receives.

The first Christmas depicted during the novel occurs after Ellen's mother has died and while she is still living with her father. She knows that she will not receive any gifts from her family. So she buys gifts for herself, things she has been wanting (the microscope, some construction paper, a pair of shoes, and a diary which locks), as well as wrapping paper for them. She happily eats a TV dinner, hides her presents, and then finds them. Ignored by her grandmother, aunts, and father, she makes her own Christmas. But she is not entirely alone, for Starletta and her parents include her in their Christmas. She is moved almost to tears by the sweater (this gift, incidentally, becomes an important moment in Ellen's beginning to overcome her racism). So through Ellen's resourcefulness and the kindness of her friend's family, this first Christmas is not as grim as it might have been, even though it comes at a grim time.

The second holiday, Ellen's eleventh birthday, is a happy moment, and once again Starletta is an important part of it. Julia and Roy remind her of the birthday she might otherwise have forgotten about, and they give her the kind of birthday "party"—a day with Starletta—that she wants. The two girls go to the movies, Starletta being the only black person there, and then the celebration, with cake, candles, and gifts, occurs in Julia's kitchen. The gifts are thoughtful and appropriate—a handmade pillow made by Starletta's mother, who makes and sells fine quilts, and much valued art supplies from Roy and Julia. But even this wonderful day is only a brief moment, for it is followed immediately by the events which lead to Ellen's removal from Roy and Julia and her placement with her grandmother. Joy is brief.

The final holiday, Christmas at her aunt Nadine's home, is the event which precipitates the novel's happy conclusion. Ellen plans for this Christmas just as carefully as she had planned for the one before, but this time she plans to make it a good Christmas for her aunt and cousin. Despite their general treatment of her as, quite literally, a poor relation, she believes they intend to give gifts to her, and she is determined that her gift to them will be worthy. Having no money to buy something appropriate, she decides to use her artistic ability and create for their home a nice picture. She carefully considers what would be pleasing to them, realizing that their taste would not allow them to appreciate "one of my brooding oceans," because they would "miss the point I am sure of how the ocean looks strong and beautiful and sad at the same time" (123), and settles on a picture of cats playing with a ball of yarn which she thinks is more to their taste. She quite perceptively recognizes their conventionality and lack of artistic understanding, and she hopes they will be impressed by and appreciative of the picture and the paper frames she has for them to choose from. (Ironically, she is as patronizing of them as her aunt is of her in her insincere praise of the picture.) Her aunt's kind but hypocritical words and her cousin's disbelief that she drew the picture herself insult and wound her deeply. When she finds that, in contrast to Dora's large number of extravagant presents, she has been given only the pack of paper for which she had specifically asked, she realizes how mistaken had been her hopes that things might be better here than they had been with her grandmother or her other aunt, and she takes action. This Christmas, bitterly disappointing for her, turns out to be the event which leads her to her final destination.

One of the most striking and important repeated images, as well as the most poetic one, in *Ellen Foster* is that of spinning. It is an appropriate image to communicate the desperation which young Ellen feels as her world repeatedly changes and seems to whirl out of her control. The feeling and meaning of this image contrast with the calmness and the practical approach to her problems which Ellen usually presents. The fact that her feelings are in turmoil even as she tries to confront repeated crises with composure is revealed through her use of this image, which is used throughout the novel at important moments. In its first occurrence, it is her comment on the way both of her parents had been defeated by their lives: "they both died," Ellen says, "tired of the wild crazy spinning and wore out and sick. . . . She sick and he drunk with the moving. They finally gave in to the motion and let the wind take them from here to there" (2–3). Defeat and despair, in Ellen's view, led to a sense of powerlessness, of loss of control, symbolized by a spinning world, and to her mother's suicide and her father's alcoholism.

After this introduction near the beginning of the novel, however, the image of spinning is applied to Ellen herself and appears at moments of crisis: at her mother's death (11), as she flees from near-rape by her father (45), as her grandmother is dying (85), and as she realizes the hopelessness of her situation with her aunts Nadine and Dora (128). It does not appear after she puts into action her plan to escape from Nadine and go to her "new mama," by its absence suggesting the new stability that she has found. No longer does she feel the world whirling around her. She has finally come to rest in a safe place.

A MARXIST READING OF *ELLEN FOSTER*

Marxist criticism, based on the political and economic theories of nineteenth-century German writer, philosopher and economist Karl Marx and his collaborator Friedrich Engels, examines the social, political, and economic conditions depicted by novelists. Marx and Engels believed that history was a struggle between wealthy and powerful classes who controlled the economic structures of society and the poor and exploited classes (the proletariat) who did the work and produced the goods and services used by the wealthy without receiving appropriate benefits for their labor. This struggle would, they believed, inevitably find its climax in the victory of the proletariat and the establishment of a classless and just society in which differences of class would be destroyed. Marxist criticism was especially influential in the United States during the Great Depression of the 1930s, when differences of class and power were made particularly obvious by the presence of great numbers of unemployed and poverty-stricken people.

In the United States, class and race are often closely linked, as many of those of African-American ancestry, descendants of former slaves, have remained poor and uneducated as a result of lack of opportunity. Thus Marxist criticism finds materials for examination in literature written about poor black people as well as in fiction depicting economic differences between people in general. Marxist writers tended to describe the desperate situations of the poor and to emphasize the differences between classes as a way of showing why a revolution is inevitable.

Although *Ellen Foster* is not a Marxist work, its subject matter makes a Marxist analysis helpful in examining it. This novel, set among poor white and black Southern Americans, depicts the poverty of members of both races and, at the same time, reveals how they are kept apart by racial divisions. Race and class work together to maintain their subordinate position. As poor as Ellen's father is, he proudly insists that he is better than the black men who are his drinking companions. As desperate as Ellen's situation is while she lives with her abusive and alcoholic father, she finds some sense of worth in her belief that she is at least better than Starletta and her parents. Her scorn for them, a Marxist critic would argue, is a defensive mechanism for her and an indirect method of ensuring that she will not see that both her and their interests are actually similar.

But Ellen does have some insights that a Marxist reader would agree with. She observes that Starletta's mother, who makes quilts and sells them, does not receive what she should from her work. Others, white middle-class urban women, buy them from her and then sell them for large profits (36). This is a classic Marxist insight, that the producers of value in a capitalist society are not those who are enriched; rather, those who already have wealth acquire more wealth by their power over the workers. Even the early and racist Ellen, because she is fair-minded and fond of Starletta and her people, recognizes the injustice here. This first mention of the misappropriation of Starletta's mother's quilts is placed within one of Ellen's early analyses of her racial feelings about Starletta's family, her scorn for them because their poorly built home is impossible to keep clean. At this point, Ellen does not allow herself to realize that their living conditions are not their choice but rather the result of their membership in an exploited underclass.

Later, when Ellen is forced to work in the fields with her grandmother's African-American field "hands," she recognizes that her grandmother's exploitation of them is unjust. She gradually becomes tanned from the hot sun, and comments that after she "toughened up" she "could pass for colored" (77), a symbolic indication that she is now one with the other exploited people with whom she is laboring. And like her, they do not receive what their work is worth. She says that her grandmother "did not pay them doodly-squat," just as she did not pay Ellen "a cent except room and board" (78). Her realization of her equality with Mavis and the others is an important step in Ellen's maturation and development of nonracist attitudes.

At the end of the novel, as Ellen is examining her newly color-blind racial attitudes and her intention to make things right with Starletta, she again comments on Starletta's mother's quilts. Her understanding of this injustice has been deepened, and now she lists it along with a number of other wrongs which have unfairly set her apart from Starletta (145). She now rejects her former thinking which used many of these evidences of discrimination as ways of reinforcing her belief in her superiority to Starletta because of her race. Now she comes to admire Starletta and her family because their lives are so difficult. She now can see herself and her friend as truly equal in worth and can admire Starletta because Starletta "had the hardest row to hoe" (146).

A Marxist critic would have difficulty with the essentially optimistic tone of the ending. Gibbons has emphasized Ellen's growth in maturity and the happy ending of the novel relates to her moving into a middle-class life with her new family, as well as in becoming, in her own mind, reconciled with Starletta by admitting her past injustices to and misunderstandings of her friend. Thus the novel's ending does not emphasize class struggle and avoids calling for the class warfare which a Marxist critic would argue is the only real solution to the injustice and discrimination depicted in the novel. Thus the ending of the novel undercuts its social and political meaning by implying that revolution is not necessary because social mobility upward is possible, and reconciliation between the races is reachable.

4

A Virtuous Woman
(1989)

Gibbons followed her first success with *Ellen Foster* two years later with another success. The new novel, *A Virtuous Woman*, however, was not uniformly so favorably received; its concluding chapter was particularly criticized. It is similar to its predecessor in setting, in use of colloquial Southern speech for its narration, in allowing central characters to tell their own story, and in its overall positive tone despite much darkness in its subject matter. Here again Gibbons uses the theme of a marriage between social unequals in which a woman marries a man below her own station in life. Differences between the two novels are equally obvious, however. Here there are two stories, for husband and wife alternately tell the story from their very different perspectives. And here instead of being a terrible mistake and leading to disaster, this marriage is happy from the point of view of both partners, and the only disaster is the untimely death of one of the couple.

The careful reader of *A Virtuous Woman* may be surprised to discover some information relating to characters from *Ellen Foster*. In the second novel, mention is made of a Ruth Hartley who takes in orphaned girls (99). One of those girls is named Ellen, and it may be surmised that these folks are Ellen Foster and her foster mother. There is in the locality the remnants of a family, now in decline, formerly of some wealth, named Butler, and a matriarch, now dead, who was in life particularly malicious and who answers to the description of Ellen's grandmother. Additionally, the old Butler woman had employed an African American, here named Mavis Washington but presumably the kindly field hand referred to only as Mavis in the earlier novel. Her characterization, however, varies markedly in the two novels. Nevertheless, her name would seem to be another clue that there is a relationship in place and time between the two books.

TITLE AND EPIGRAPH

The title of *A Virtuous Woman* is taken from a well-known passage in Proverbs (31:10–25) which describes the qualities of "a virtuous woman." It touches on the woman's economic value to her husband through her labor, her value to the community through her charitable efforts, the honor she brings to her family through her actions, and her joy in her situation. The novel, using one example, describes the life of a woman who is considered just such a virtuous woman despite her unconventional behavior in some respects. Both title and biblical passage are very significant and must be taken into account in any careful consideration of this novel. The text from Proverbs is a familiar one but is nevertheless quoted in full as the epigraph to Gibbons's novel. Its opening lines read:

> A virtuous woman who can find?
> For her price is far above rubies.
> The heart of her husband trusteth in her,
> And he shall have no lack of gain.
> She doeth him good and not evil
> All the days of her life.

The passage then lists such a woman's qualities and deeds. They suggest her value in economic and familial terms: she cares for her family and home, and she brings both honor and financial profit to her family. It is noteworthy that both the novel's title and its title character's name are taken from the first two lines above, for it is surely not coincidental that the virtuous woman of this story is named "Ruby." Also, the focus on home and family suggested in the biblical quotation is maintained throughout the novel, and Ruby is seen principally as a wife whose value is measured by her relationship to her husband and by what she contributes to their marriage. Some of the details disagree, for Ruby's labors never bring worldly wealth to her husband, nor does she help to make him a highly respected and powerful figure in his community, unlike the "virtuous woman" of Proverbs. Nevertheless, the epigraph, along with the title, sets up for the reader one purpose of the novel, that of examining what a virtuous woman might be in the late-twentieth-century American South. However, title and epigraph are misleading in that the novel seems as much about the woman's effect on her husband and about the quality of their relationship as it is directly about the woman. Thematically, then, the novel is more complicated than title and epigraph, important as they are, initially suggest.

NARRATIVE METHOD

As in *Ellen Foster*, Gibbons chose to use a first-person narrative method, that is, to have her story told by a participant in its action. However, her method in *A Virtuous Woman* is more elaborate than in the earlier novel. Here she uses two narrators, her two main characters, who tell the story in alternating chapters. The novel opens in the narrative of Jack Stokes, the husband of the title character, who speaks in the first and in succeeding odd-numbered chapters. The second and following even-numbered chapters are, in the narrative of Ruby, the virtuous woman. The concluding chapter breaks this pattern, for as the novel is being summed up and brought to a conclusion, Gibbons turns to a third-person narrative. This final portion of the novel is told by an omniscient narrator, an outside and objective voice who is able to understand all characters and events fully and therefore to sum them up authoritatively. It also includes the thoughts of four important characters as the novelist brings a measure of closure to the events of the story.

The main portion of the novel, told alternatively by Jack and Ruby, gives the first and the last word to him, opening, as he tells readers in his first sentence, by indicating that his wife has been dead for four months and closing as he tries desperately to feel her continuing presence with him. His narrative is firmly placed in the months after her death. Because the novel begins after its central character is dead and makes use of her narration, some reviewers have been puzzled by its placement in time, assuming that she is somehow speaking from beyond the grave. However, its placement is in fact during the months between her diagnosis with terminal lung cancer and her death.

The two narrators are sharply distinguished from each other in their language (Ruby speaks mostly in standard English, whereas Jack's language is full of Southern dialect and unconventional grammar). Jack, uneducated as he is, tends also to be rather shallow in his thought, not trying to examine feelings or ideas in any depth, whereas Ruby is more concerned to understand the meanings of events. A reader can open the novel to any page and know very quickly whose narrative is there because of the clear and obvious differences between their narrative styles.

The shift in point of view in the last chapter was a risky move by the author. As Stephen Souris points out, it may be seen either as successfully bringing closure to what would otherwise be an unsettling duality of focus or as unsuccessfully departing from a very effective balancing of two separate points of view on the same materials (110–12).

PLOT AND STRUCTURE

A Virtuous Woman, like *Ellen Foster*, is based on the premise of a woman marrying down, and it might be considered a threefold narrative. It is in part the story of the life of Ruby Pitt Woodrow Stokes, in part the story of the life of her husband, "Blinking" Jack Ernest Stokes, and in part the story of their marriage. Thus despite the title which directs readers' attention to Ruby as the title character, there might be considered to be two protagonists, or central characters, both Ruby and Jack. Title and epigraph focus on Ruby, but emphasis is directed to Jack by the facts that Jack speaks first and last and that Ruby is dead when Jack's narrative takes place, a major part of his story being his attempt to consider how he can live on after he has lost her. His narrative, then, tells the story of his life and of his point of view on his marriage to Ruby as he attempts to understand his situation after her death. Ruby's narrative describes her life before she met Jack and explains how she came to marry him, as well as discussing their marriage. She is speaking much more closely in time to the events she describes, perhaps a necessary function of the fact that her death has been revealed in the very first line of the novel. All this complicates the way in which the events of the novel are presented. In *Ellen Foster*, Gibbons worked back and forth between two periods in the life of one central character, while maintaining that character's point of view throughout. In *A Virtuous Woman*, in contrast, she works back and forth between the present and the past of two different characters, alternating between their separate interpretations of what they have experienced, and then finally stepping out of those two points of view to present other notions as the characters remaining after Ruby's death must move on.

Several distinct plot lines can be observed running through the narrative. There are the separate stories of the lives of Ruby and Jack which merge into the story of their marriage. The life stories of Ruby and Jack are told in their narratives of their pasts as each tries to come to an understanding of their marriage and of how Ruby's death will affect Jack's future. Both characters tell not only their own stories but also present their understanding of the past of the other, and both tell from their own perspective what their marital relationship has been like. The reader must pull things together, figuring out the various time lines: the separate stories of Ruby's and Jack's lives before they meet, then the single story line seen from two points of view of their marriage, and of Ruby's diagnosis of lung cancer, her subsequent death, and Jack's grief.

In brief, Ruby's story is of a rather privileged and spoiled girl who marries a migrant worker in order to escape what she sees as an unhappy existence. That first marriage turns out to be a terrible mistake, not because her husband, John Woodrow, is beneath her in social status and wealth, but because he is both alcoholic and abusive. In many respects he resembles Ellen's father in Gibbons's first novel. Ruby escapes that terrible marriage when John Woodrow, after being flagrantly unfaithful to her, dies from wounds suffered in a drunken brawl. She then marries Jack Stokes, who, like John Woodrow, is beneath her in status but who is very unlike her first husband in temperament.

Jack's story is one of poverty and deprivation, as well as of personal feelings of inferiority. A tenant farmer, he has never owned much of anything, and his marriage to Ruby is the best thing that ever happens to him. When they marry, their stories merge, and the story of their marriage, told from their contrasting points of view, shows it to have been a successful relationship, bringing fulfillment to both of them. When Ruby's lung cancer is diagnosed and her approaching death is made clear, the story becomes one of his denial and her preparations for his meals after her death.

CHARACTER DEVELOPMENT

Even though the focus in the novel is divided between Ruby and Jack, the title and the epigram direct special attention to Ruby, and it is really her presence, not Jack's, on which the novel is based. She was the youngest child and the pampered daughter of middle-class propertied parents. She thinks, in looking back, that her parents overprotected her, prevented her from making mistakes, and therefore kept her from learning from mistakes. They made choices for her, and they reared her in a very traditional home. A particularly telling detail is that they "always used cloth napkins, company or no company" (28). Ruby's father is a man of prominence in the county, serving several terms as a county commissioner and known to everyone (28). The family has a couple, Sudie Bee and Lester, who live in an apartment adjoining their house and who are almost as much parts of the family as they are servants. She stresses that while her family did not teach her much about the world and about making sensible choices, they did teach her self-respect (29).

But little of this helps her when she meets John Woodrow (he is always referred to by his full name), a migrant worker who comes to labor in her father's fields. The family, against the advice of wise Sudie Bee, invites the migrants into their home to use the bathroom and eat the luncheon served to them, only to discover that the workers have trashed their house. Ruby's mother's illusions are destroyed by this experience and she does not again face the laborers, but protected and idealistic Ruby somehow seems to believe she can relate to these men. As she sums it up, "instead of running away from it . . . I rushed to it and tried to forgive and understand it" (33).

In brief, Ruby elopes with John Woodrow, only to be quickly disillusioned. She soon realizes that his criticisms of her family as "too uppity, too picky, and way, way too rich" (33) are incorrect, for her father had worked hard to achieve what the family had and they are very careful in budgeting their resources. She also realizes that he has lied to her, falsely claiming to have been badly treated and cheated out of an inheritance by a family not unlike her own. She realizes that marrying him has been a horrible mistake. Instead of the marriage raising her husband to her level, it lowers her to his. She is very aware of the difference between the two worlds of her former and her present life. She hates the rootless life of a migrant crew, and she is shamed and hurt by his psychological and physical abuse. The shame is apparently what keeps her from fleeing home. She tries to explain why she never left John Woodrow to return to her parents: "I thought about it a hundred times a day. Sometimes that was all I had to think about except how my body hurt. What would I have said? 'Daddy, did you ever hear of *Tobacco Road?* Well, the situation I'm in is a lot like that, only we're moving from place to place and I'm never sure where I am. So next summer when the migrants sit under our sycamore tree, don't think of anyone else but me.' " (34–35).

The allusions in the above quotation are of some interest. In mentioning *Tobacco Road*, Ruby is showing her familiarity with the novel by Erskine Caldwell which portrayed the lives of the sort of people often called "poor white trash" in the South, landless and ignorant sharecroppers and tenant farmers whose lives are full of violence. Less obvious to young readers today, probably, is the reference to a popular song from the era of the World War II, a song in which a departing soldier tells his sweetheart not to sit under an apple tree with anyone else until he returns from overseas. The fact of her finding it natural to speak in such allusions separates her from both John Woodrow and Jack Stokes, neither of whom would have caught the references—John Woodrow would not have cared, but Jack Stokes might have been a bit puzzled by them. Even her education is somewhat lacking, however, and she makes a rather obvious mistake when she refers to some familiar words of Jesus' as a psalm (115). Her comment is that the " 'In my Father's house there are many mansions' psalm" is a particularly "depressing" one. To many Christians, of course, this passage from John 14:1, not from the much more ancient Psalms, is a particularly comforting one as it introduces a promise of eternal life. For that very reason it is often used at funerals, and this fact may explain Ruby's description of it as depressing.

At any event, Ruby is trapped in a horrible marriage, but she sticks with it, until her situation becomes impossible. She becomes a maid of all work in the home of a family of property, thus falling to the position of the maid Sudie Bee whose example she tries to follow as she attempts to figure out how to perform the tasks she is set. Actually, her position is much worse than Sudie Bee's, for the latter was treated with respect, unlike Ruby in the household of the Hoover family. Ruby soon discovers John Woodrow in an act of adultery, one which he almost seems to have planned to taunt her with. Her anger and desperation are so great that she even buys a pistol, but John Woodrow disappears and soon she learns he has been cut up in a brawl in a poolroom and then that he has died of his wounds.

In her new freedom, she turns to a man she has just met, Jack Stokes, who had been the one to bring her the news of John Woodrow's death. They soon marry, despite the disparity in their ages (he is more than twice her age), and this marriage, unlike her first one, turns out very well. Each has something the other needs, and Ruby cares lovingly for

Jack. Despite their differences in background, which are no less than those between Ruby and John Woodrow, they succeed in caring for each other. Unfortunately, one thing remains with Ruby from her first marriage—the habit of smoking to which John Woodrow had introduced her. This habit leads to her early death from lung cancer, but before that occurs they make a good life for each other.

One great regret, however, mars the marriage from her point of view—her childlessness. Perhaps because John Woodrow had given her a sexually transmitted disease, she is unable to bear children, and her disappointment over this inability causes her deep pain. She partly fills the void, however, by her relationship with June, the neglected child of Tiny Fran (more about each of them later), for whose successful upbringing she is almost completely responsible. Somehow, Ruby is able to bring good from her pain.

Her love explains her concern for Jack's welfare after her death. On learning her diagnosis, her primary goal is to enable him to survive at least the first few months after her death: she fills the freezer with packages which contain complete meals, so all he must do is take them out as he needs them. She hopes to prepare enough food to last him for three months (5), but in fact these provisions are enough for four months. That she knew her husband and his needs well is shown by his comically desperate attempts to cook for himself when her supplies for him have run out (122–23).

Ruby is a thoughtful woman who puzzles over her experience and feelings and tries to figure them out. She considers her reasons for marrying both her husbands and she thinks about—and is often irritated or frustrated by—Jack's inability to be sensitive to her feelings. A major example of this occurs at the time of her diagnosis. The two meet this crisis in very different ways. He immediately denies its reality and encourages Ruby to deny it as well. But Ruby understands her mortality and needs for Jack to hold and comfort her, not simply to refuse to accept the reality of what is to come (6–7). Her understanding of and her love for him are shown by her immediate regret for lashing out at him and hurting him (7), and she then discusses an earlier parallel to their situation in the way her grandfather failed her dying grandmother. Her sensitivity and understanding here are far beyond what Jack can comprehend.

Jack is a very unlikely husband for Ruby, and he would probably never have met her were it not for her disastrous first marriage. Certainly he would never dare to speak to her if she were not a deserted and suffering young woman when he first sees her. He always considers her far above him and never stops marveling that she loves him. He is much older than she; he is a poor and ignorant tenant farmer, while she comes of landed and educated people; he is scrawny and unattractive while she is lovely; and he is lacking in sensitivity and perceptivity while she has both of these qualities. In just about every way, they would seem to be mismatched. And she often is frustrated by his inability to see what she understands or to sense her feelings. But nevertheless his good qualities are valuable. He is steady and loving, and he takes care of her. He always cherishes her, and he becomes dependent on her emotional support, as well as her physical care for him. The depth of his love is suggested by his emotional collapse at her death.

Jack presents himself as what can only be called a loser, and that is clearly how he thinks of himself. He is very aware of the great disparity in age between him and Ruby (she is twenty to his forty-five when they marry), and he admits that the reason he has waited so long to marry is that he knows (or believes) that no one wanted him. But before he sees Ruby, he has never attempted to court a woman. He is sure that Ruby sees him as a worthless man, and he realizes that she "wanted somebody to take care of her" (41). It is his love for Ruby and his willingness to protect her that give him the courage to approach her. And he always feels that it is her love for him that teaches him "what it must feel like to be a man" (42). His sense of inferiority to her and his amazement that she condescends to marry him remain with him throughout the twenty-five years of their marriage (she is forty-five when she dies).

It is not only Jack's appearance that he believes is against him. He is uneducated, the son of a Holiness man and a part Cherokee woman. He drinks too much. His family never has any land, and until the end of *A Virtuous Woman*, he has no property, only the land he farms as a tenant first to Lonnie Hoover and then to Burr Stanley. His lack of education is shown in his narratives, which contrast markedly with Ruby's, both in their uncertain grammar and their inability to make (or lack of interest in) any very deep analysis of feelings and relationships. It is the latter characteristic which is most frustrating to Ruby, who repeatedly complains of his lack of sensitivity and then makes excuses for him.

But Jack's good qualities are for Ruby—and for readers—far more important than his flaws. He is warm and loving, and he is steadfast. Despite his lack of interest in analyzing relationships, he builds lasting ones. He cares tenderly for Ruby, and he mourns her bitterly after she is gone. He farms the same land his whole adult life, even though he has no stake in it, and he deals fairly with his first landlord, Lonnie Hoover, even though he comments scornfully on Hoover's family. He thinks of Burr almost as his son, and their long-lasting friendship is strong and enriching to both men.

Happy as he is in his marriage to Ruby, there are two things lacking. The first is children, who are more important to Ruby, although like her he feels an incompleteness. Typically for him, he accepts the responsibility for their childlessness, just because he generally feels that "if it was something wrong going on it was me that caused it. And it was" (98). His blunt statement in those last three words is particularly telling, and he insists that the responsibility must be his even though in the same paragraph he repeats two other possible explanations: Ruby's that she is infertile because of a sexually transmitted disease, and the doctor's that these things happen. Despite what both Ruby and the doctor tell him, his simple certainty that he must be to blame remains with him.

Jack also has the idea of taking in an orphan, someone like Ellen Foster, but he discards this idea because he fears he is not good enough to be approved by the state. So when Ruby and June, Burr's daughter with Tiny Fran, become close, he rejoices in the child's filling some of the emptiness in their marriage and cherishes June just as he does Ruby. Like Ruby, however, he always regrets that they did not have a child of their own, because as much as they love June she is still the daughter of others, to whom they must defer.

Jack's other regret, not really connected to their marriage or to Ruby, is his landlessness. To him, however, the two lacks are connected. In his grief for Ruby's death, he thinks of his own mortality and sees his lack of children and land as meaning that he will have no immortality. He loves the land he farms, but as a tenant he always feels insecure. He considers that his love for and use of the land over many years have given him a moral right to it, but he wishes deeply to have that moral right upheld by a legal deed. When Lonnie Hoover dies, some ten years before Ruby's death, Jack allows himself to hope that Lonnie has willed to Jack the land that Jack has lived on all his life. He remembers how his own father was killed in a tractor accident for which he blames Lonnie's father (58–60). He believes that the Hoover family owes him something for that loss, but he is not surprised that no such stipulation is found in Lonnie's will. He knows he has been foolish to have hopes, but he is nevertheless keenly disappointed.

He could have had land, for Ruby's parents leave their land to be divided between her and her two brothers. But that is not his land, and so he refuses it, and with Ruby's agreement it is divided simply between her brothers (55–56). His longing for land is real, but what he wants is the land he knows and loves and has worked for his entire life. After Ruby's death, Burr gives that land to him. When he offers, Jack accepts this land, and although he reminds himself that the land will not replace Ruby, the gift is the beginning of his acceptance of her death and his building a life without her.

In many ways, Jack is a character of pathos, one readers might be tempted to pity. However, his love, endurance, persistence, and strength are admirable and create sympathy for him. In one way neither of his great desires is given to him, at least not in the way that would have been most meaningful to him: much though he and Ruby love June, she is not their own child, and the land he longs to have as his own is withheld from him until after the death of the woman with whom he would have wanted to share it. While he is very aware of what he does not have (children and land of his own), he is also aware that he does have compensations (June's love and, finally, the land so long belonging to others). His virtues are rewarded, although with limitations.

Contrasted with the happy marriage of Ruby and Jack, who meet each other's needs and love each other, is the union of Tiny Fran and Burr, who marry because they seem at the time to meet each other's immediate needs but who do not love each other. In addition, Tiny Fran is the very opposite of a "virtuous woman." The spoiled daughter of Lonnie Hoover and his doting wife Frances, Tiny Fran is about Ruby's age but is fat, self-centered, and sexually promiscuous. When Ruby goes to work as a maid in the Hoover household, Tiny Fran shows her no respect (contrasting with the respect shown by Ruby's family for Sudie Bee), and by being lazy and demanding makes Ruby's life even more difficult than it otherwise might have been. She is shamelessly pregnant but the father of her child remains unknown, and her father arranges her marriage to Burr by bribing him with a gift of land. Knowing what Tiny Fran is like, Burr (like Jack, then a landless tenant farmer) accepts the bribe.

Throughout the novel, Tiny Fran remains self-centered, thoughtless, and cruel. She dotes on Roland, the child whose conception forced her marriage and who turns out badly, partly no doubt because of her terrible parenting. She neglects and abuses June, the child of her marriage to Burr, but resents Ruby's relationship with her daughter and does what she can to disrupt it. When her marriage to Burr ends in divorce, Burr buys her share of the land from her, but when that money runs out, for she lives expensively and foolishly, he makes her an allowance—and is happy to do so as it keeps her out of his life.

If Tiny Fran is a horrid example of what a woman should not be, unlike Ruby, Burr is in some respects much like a younger version of Jack without Jack's sense of inferiority. He comes from several generations of tenant farmers, and it is his lack of land of his own that leads him to marry Tiny Fran. He longs so deeply for his own land that this bribe makes up for his sacrifice. The two men are close, Jack thinking of Burr as almost like a son. Their relationship continues throughout the novel, with Burr doing what he can for Jack but finally feeling helpless in the face of Jack's great loss. In the end of the novel, he finally does what he perhaps should have done much earlier when he gives Jack's land to him. If anyone should have understood Jack's yearning for full legal possession of his farm, it should have been Burr, but somehow he does not act on that knowledge until he sees Jack's great grief for his dead wife and tries to find some way to help him. He means well, and he finally makes this most meaningful gift.

June, Tiny Fran and Burr's daughter, is as important for what she represents as for who she actually is. Neglected by her mother, she is taken in hand and loved by Ruby, and it is Ruby's nurturing her that is probably at least partly responsible for her success. From a troubled childhood in which she is ill-treated by her mother and physically abused by her malicious and cruel older brother (who later goes from animal abuse to rape and is sent to prison), she becomes a college graduate and architect employed by a firm in a nearby city. In the novel's concluding chapter, she comforts Jack and tries to care for him in his grief, cleaning his house and trying to understand the bizarre behavior into which his pain leads him. She also grieves for Ruby herself, comparing her with her birth mother and wishing that Ruby, not Tiny Fran, had been her parent. Her love for her surrogate parents, both the suffering Jack and the dead Ruby, is deep and clear, but so also are her love for Burr, her actual father, and her scorn for Tiny Fran. June has turned out to be a strong and sensitive young professional woman, and much of the credit for her success can go to Ruby.

A number of lesser characters are present, among them John Woodrow (Ruby's ne'er-do-well and abusive first husband), Frances Hoover (Lonnie Hoover's wife and Tiny Fran's mother), and Roland Hoover (June's criminal brother). These characters play minor roles in the action and have some effects on the central characters. Two other characters who play minor roles but create some comic relief merit brief mention. One is Cecil Spangler, pastor at the Ephesus Free Will Baptist Church, a religious literalist who tries to convert Jack to his fundamentalist faith out of all the best motives but who is mocked by Jack in their arguments over theology and the Bible. Cecil becomes comic because of the way he takes everything literally and his inability to see the flaws in his arguments.

The other of these minor characters is Mavis Washington, who may or may not be seen as the kindly field hand of *Ellen Foster*. The Mavis in this novel, however, is a purely comic character, fat and lazy, who hires herself out as housekeeper and cook to Jack in the days after Ruby's frozen food runs out. She spends her days at his house flopped in her chair, watching his television, and complaining about her bad knees. When she finally does some work, she ruins his jeans by putting too much bleach in the laundry. This comic passage (127–34) emphasizes Jack's desperation, for it is surprising that he would even consider having her in his house. It may also be troubling to many readers, for it may be considered to play upon an unfortunate stereotype, that of the black mammy.

SETTING

The comments made about settings in *Ellen Foster* (see chapter 3) hold true also for *A Virtuous Woman*. Once again, the setting in the rural South is basic to everything in the novel, and yet once again it is not dwelt upon or specifically developed. It appears in the lives and idioms of the characters and in their behavior and in the things they take for granted. Their Southern way of life is for them simply the way things are, and they do not particularly think about it. Tobacco farming as a way of life, fundamentalist Christian beliefs centered around a Baptist congregation, a class system based on race and landholding or landlessness, some particular ways of speaking—all these, present without comment in Gibbons's text, reveal and regularly remind readers of the rural Southern context in which the events of the novel take place.

As noted earlier, there are some specific relationships in the contexts of *Ellen Foster* and *A Virtuous Woman*. Several references in *A Virtuous Woman* to a person who is clearly the Ellen of the previous novel indicate that Ruby's death occurs after Ellen has found her home with her foster family. Thus it may be placed in the period after the late 1970s. However, the later novel adds to the information about setting which readers can glean from the earlier one. As Ruby and Jack are adult narrators, they tend to be more aware than was Ellen Foster of the community and institutions around them, and so there are more specific references to place names. "Ephesus" is referred to several times (see, for instance, pages 76, 91, 114), but it is unclear whether this is the name of a town or of a church, and the Ephesus Free Will Baptist Church (109) is specified as the name of the congregation, which is clearly the one through which Ellen met her foster mother, as well as the one which Jack refuses to attend.

Two other place names occur: Shelbourne (148), the town where June is a practicing architect at the time of the latest events in *A Virtuous Woman* and, more specifically, Georgia, presumably giving readers a final clear indication as to where Gibbons's first two novels are placed (125). Neither reference, however, is especially helpful in giving clarity to the settings, and the truly important information is that which is taken for granted by the narrators, giving the novels their texture as stories of Southern poor white who know no other place.

LANGUAGE AND STYLE

As in *Ellen Foster*, Gibbons manages her narrative with great skill. Her two narrators both speak in very personal idioms, each expressing ideas in a way that is special to that speaker. Neither is highly educated, although Ruby has done enough reading to make some literary allusions, as noted previously. Her speech is generally grammatical and thoughtful, with some use of imagery and a good deal of analysis of thoughts and feelings. Jack's narrative makes no pretenses to education and is, in fact, full of nonstandard usages, which give evidence both of his lack of education and of his Southern roots. A few examples will serve to illustrate. On several occasions he uses a verb construction which will seem strange to non-Southern readers: "might would could've." He says, for example, that imagining their own child would have turned out as well as June did is "an awful lot to pretend like what might would could've happened" (99). This heaping up of verb forms seems to intensify the uncertainty or doubt he is expressing. Other turns of phrase which help to characterize Jack's narrative are simply nonstandard grammar, as when he mixes up the case of his pronouns and the form of his verbs: "My daddy always was a Holiness man, always trying to shove Jesus down I and mama's throats. He drug me to church and tent revivals" (14). "I and mama" contains two "errors"—nominative case when objective is demanded, and placement of the first-person pronoun before a reference to a second person, although primary teachers have long insisted that "I" or "me" in compound constructions should always come second. Additionally, of course, "drug" as the past tense of "drag" is generally considered a nonstandard usage.

THEMES

Death and dying are obviously a central theme for this novel, which traces the dying of a woman and its effects on her husband, and in fact much of the preceding discussion of the novel is also a discussion of this theme. Therefore, perhaps a little more needs to be said about it here. However, it is interesting to note the way in which the theme of death is linked with the means of Ruby's death: tobacco and smoking. Tobacco is the cash crop of the region in which these characters live, and it is the crop Jack grows. The use of tobacco is introduced to Ruby by her first husband, John Woodrow, and is the only thing of his she retains after his death, for by then she is addicted to smoking. Sadly, the use that she had taken up as a kind of defense mechanism during that first unhappy marriage stays with her and eventually kills her. Jack and Ruby's meeting and their final parting, at her death, are both associated with tobacco. When Jack first sees Ruby, she is smoking, and it is ironic that his first words to her are to criticize her for using tobacco, his own crop. Her last gesture as she is dying is to ask him for a cigarette, emphasizing the power of her addiction. Thus, her use of tobacco, the substance which had been their livelihood but which ironically also kills her, frames the story.

Another interesting theme is that of religious belief, or perhaps better, nonbelief. Despite their differing backgrounds, Jack and Ruby have come to very similar conclusions about religion, both of them denying its validity and refusing to have anything to do with the church. Jack engages in long arguments on theology and the Bible with Cecil Spangler, and Ruby thoughtfully discusses her reasons for not believing in God, although she expresses belief in some kind of afterlife (112–13). The tones of their comments on faith—and lack of it—are rather different. Ruby is thoughtful, while Jack is angry and scornful. When Jack talks with Cecil Spangler, he is taunting, and in his narrative, when he might be assumed to be thinking his ideas through, he mocks some Judeo-Christian elements of faith. A favorite line of his, given twice, is a contemptuous allusion to a familiar biblical line: "Think about that, O ye of all that faith!" (92; only the last portion repeated, 111).

He finds reason for his rejection of religious faith in his personal understanding of biblical stories. For example, God's promise to Noah not to again destroy the world, as had happened after the Flood and is symbolized by the rainbow, strikes Jack as simply cruel. He uses a very earthy illustration to explain his point of view: "How would you like it if I slammed your fingers in the car door . . . and I said, 'Oh, let me make it up to you. Here's a quarter and I promise I won't ever do it again'?" (91–92). As his narrative is occurring after Ruby's death, some of his anger may be related to his pain at her death, but his rejection of religious faith comes from his way of seeing the world, not just from his grief.

Ruby's expressions of nonbelief are more thoughtful, as is usual for her. She regrets Jack's rudeness to Cecil Spangler, saying her husband has been turned "mean and malicious," quite different from his usual self (111). Unlike Jack, she does not look for logical reasons to reject religious faith. Instead she simply states that she and Jack don't think Cecil's worldview is valid. She continues to speak for Jack as well as for herself when she comments that for her, the existence of the world is miracle enough. And she denies feeling anger at her approaching death. Unlike Jack, she accepts it as inevitable and says that for her, the main emotion is not rage but rather regret at what she will miss. And she goes on to speak for both of them, saying that they believe that there is some kind of continuance after death. She believes that her spirit, having separated from her body, will join the spirits of family members who have already died, and so she, and Jack as well, she says, do maintain a kind of belief in immortality. She quotes Jack as saying that the soul, after death, will " 'do anything it damn well pleases' " (113), but Jack himself does not directly express this idea. Her calm acceptance of her death and his contrasting denial and pain relate to the quiet thoughtfulness of her comments on faith and his bitter rejection of religious belief. This sharp distinction between the statements on faith of her two central characters is one of many ways in which Gibbons differentiates between their voices, and it also illustrates how two people with basically similar ideas on religion may nevertheless react very differently.

Only one other major theme needs to be discussed here, the theme of marriage. It is very clear through the presentation of the marriage of Jack and Ruby as they separately tell their joint story that this theme is central to the novel. It is enriched by the presentation of another marriage which sharply contrasts with it, that of Tiny Fran and Burr. Although both couples marry in part for reasons which are at least questionable (Ruby needing the protection and support Jack can give her rather than loving her, Tiny Fran needing to give her expected baby a name and a father, and Burr wanting the land promised him by Tiny Fran's father), one marriage works, and the other is a terrible failure. The reasons for marriage of Tiny Fran and Burr are more selfish and worldly than those of Ruby and Jack, and additionally Ruby is indeed a virtuous woman, prepared to care for and nurture her husband, unlike Tiny Fran who remains self-centered and demanding, unable to concern herself with anyone else's needs. Tiny Fran and Burr have the two things Ruby and Jack long for, children and land, yet the more fortunate mother is unable to cherish her daughter and ruins her son by her favoritism. Burr never regrets marrying for the land, but its possession does not save or enrich his marriage, and although he does love his daughter, he is unable to protect her from the cruelty and neglect of her mother. The marriage ends in divorce, but not until after the less fortunate couple has rescued June, Burr and Tiny Fran's daughter, and given her the love her mother will not. Through her innate "virtuous" qualities of loving and nurturing, Ruby builds a good marriage and rescues an abused girl.

But all the blame is not Tiny Fran's for her failed marriage, nor is all the credit for Ruby's success her own. Burr never loves, in fact never respects, Tiny Fran, and everyone knows from the beginning that she is pregnant by another unknown man and that Burr is marrying her for the land her father can give him. His scorn for his wife does not exactly make him a good husband to her, although there seems little reason to think that it makes any real difference. And Jack contributes greatly to the success of his marriage by loving and caring for Ruby, by fulfilling her needs in a way that Burr never considers trying to do for Tiny Fran. Neither marriage and none of the marriage partners are shown as totally good or as completely guilty in causing the success of one and the failure of the other marriage—although it is hard to find much good to say of Tiny Fran. Like John Woodrow, Ruby's abusive first husband, Tiny Fran is an almost completely evil character, and along with him she demonstrates the worst that can happen in a marriage.

A FEMINIST READING OF *A VIRTUOUS WOMAN*

Literary criticism takes as its goal the illumination of the meanings of works of literature, including, of course, fiction. Among other functions, it examines themes and other aspects of the literary works to explore the ways in which they comment on the actual world. Feminist literary criticism, as one approach to fiction, concentrates on the meanings of works of literature which relate to women, particularly to their roles and functions in society. Writers of feminist criticism vary widely in their political views of appropriate means for women to achieve positions of true equality in society, but they agree that women have throughout history been oppressed and that among the achievements of feminist authors have been pointing out this oppression, suggesting ways of coping with it or changing it, praising accomplishments women have made despite this oppression, and suggesting what the proper sphere of women might be. Traditional literature, written mostly by men, and traditional literary criticism, also written mostly by men, have tended to ignore women or trivialize their concerns. Female characters are fewer than male, and their issues, themes, roles, and ideas are less often examined in literary works than are those of women. Literary criticism long tended to ignore these omissions.

Women writers and feminist literary critics have attempted to add balance. Women writers, especially of recent years, have tried to do this by imagining women in various situations and by centering their works around female characters. Writers of feminist literary works sometimes depict strong women who succeed despite obstacles placed in their way by an unsympathetic society or by the men with whom they must relate. They show women successfully taking on unfamiliar or untraditional roles. But sometimes they portray weak women or women unable to withstand oppressive treatment. In either case, the emphasis is often on women themselves, not on the men who have more traditionally been the subjects of literary treatment, and the works show how the fact of their gender has affected the lives of the women. Feminist criticism then analyzes the creations of these writers, relating their fictions to reality and its meaning to real women in the real world.

Simply because of its title and biblical epigraph, *A Virtuous Woman* invites feminist analysis. It takes a woman and her life and concerns as central to its story, and thus far it seems to be feminist. But questions need to be asked about the definition of "virtue" which the novel seems to support. It is clear that the novel depicts a woman who lives out her life in a traditional sphere. She is a wife, twice in fact, and never seriously seeks to be independent or to do anything on her own. Ruby never sees any role for herself except that of wife, and the great disappointment of her life is that she is never able to take on the other traditional role for a woman, that of mother. She cooks and cleans house and cares for her husband, and not having her own child, she nurtures the child of another woman, a woman who is a total failure in the traditional roles of women.

These arguments might seem to suggest that *A Virtuous Woman* is not only not a feminist novel but also is an antifeminist work. However, most readers probably do not come away from the novel feeling that it is truly antifeminist. In fact, some feminist readers might begin to be bothered by the possibly antifeminist elements of the novel only as they begin to examine its themes after they have read it. The reason for this possible difference between emotional response to the novel and intellectual analysis of it is probably to be found simply in Ruby's strength and perseverance.

Ruby is a believable character and an admirable one. She does not have an easy life, but it is a life lived by principles and by love. After making the foolish and impulsive mistake of marrying John Woodrow, she accepts the consequences. She does not return, weakly, to her family, and she learns with grace to do hard physical work. She sees that Jack Stokes is far from the sort of man—in age, education, social class, and wealth—she might have married had she not made that first terrible mistake. But she also sees that he is a good man and that with him she will be able to live something like the life she wants. In other words, she makes her own choices and accepts the results of those choices. When she is unable to have a child, she once again is strong. She accepts the likelihood that the infertility is likely hers, not Jack's, and although she blames it on her having caught a sexually transmitted disease from John Woodrow, she does not dwell on it. Instead, she finds an outlet for her thwarted maternal desires by loving little June and giving her the strong role model that enables June to grow up to become a less traditional woman than she is herself. June's profession of architect brings into the novel a more obviously feminist note than we have otherwise been observing, but it might be argued that the strength that has enabled her to enter that traditionally masculine field is not really terribly different from the strength that enabled Ruby to find fulfillment in her unusual marriage and surrogate motherhood. June will have a better life than either

her mother or Ruby, rescued by Ruby from her mother's selfishness, malice, and frivolity, and strengthened by Ruby to make her own choices and make them more wisely than did Ruby herself. Finally, then, *A Virtuous Woman* may be seen as a novel which is feminist in a somewhat unexpected way.

5

A Cure for Dreams
(1991)

Gibbons's third novel, like its predecessors, was favorably received by
reviewers. It is a departure in some respects from her earlier work but
also shows continuity with the preceding books. Again she plays with
a first-person narrative, and again she centers her story on female experience. Again the setting is the rural South, and the characters are
neither highly educated nor wealthy. In this novel, however, there are
four women, four generations of the same family, whose lives and experiences are involved, although to quite varying degrees. The narrative, instead of coming directly from a protagonist, is filtered through
the voices of two of the women. Several marriages are depicted, but
they are not obviously examples of women "marrying down," as had
been seen in both earlier novels. Once again, events are episodic rather
than being tied tightly in a clear plotline, but here the events carry
readers over an extended span of time, from the life of the great-
grandmother to the time of the story's frame, in the voice of the great-
granddaughter. Geographic setting is also more varied, for unlike the
earlier novels which were limited to one small part of the rural American South, this novel also makes some use of settings in Kentucky,
Ireland, and Richmond. As in *Ellen Foster* but not in *A Virtuous Woman*,
male characters are presented principally for their impact on the
women of the story.

NARRATIVE METHOD

The complexities of the narrative method of *A Cure for Dreams* are introduced in the novel's opening sentence. A short, single page, printed in italics and consisting of three paragraphs (the third is only one line which has two brief sentences), in form like a letter with a date and signature, begins by giving readers three names and their family descent. The writer is Marjorie Polly Randolph, she says, and she identifies her mother as Betty Davies Randolph and her mother's mother as Lottie O'Cadhain Davies. Bridget, the fourth, and oldest, of the women whose experience will be the subject of the novel, does not appear until the narrative is underway. The introduction, as will be seen later, also presents a central theme of the novel, that of talking, of conversation, and storytelling.

This introduction, or prologue, dated December 15, 1989, is paired with a concluding page (171), which is in form just like the first. It is also in italics, carries the same date, and once again is signed, as is the opening, by Marjorie's initials. This conclusion, or epilogue, carries four paragraphs, the last of which is only one sentence long and runs a single word more than one line. It gives a few details about events occurring after the main narrative and mentions again the writer's mother and grandmother, although again the great-grandmother is not named. The theme of talking is again highlighted.

The narration of the novel is more complicated than the introduction would seem to promise. All of the nineteen chapters of the main narrative are introduced with quotation marks, and all are in the voice of Marjorie's mother, Betty, at first as she tells Marjorie stories which her mother Lottie had earlier told her and later as she tells her own story. Some readers may be confused by this presentation and have to disentangle the various narrators and generations and relationships involved. Assistance is given by chapter headings which, in the style of nineteenth-century novels and in third-person narrative, give clues as to which characters and events are the actual subjects of the chapter in question. For example, the heading for the first chapter reads, *"What passed between Lottie O'Cadhain and Charles Davies in their beginning"* (3).

A further complexity is added by the use of italics from time to time when Lottie, the subject of Betty's narrative as quoted by Marjorie, is quoted by Betty. Thus statements made by one character are quoted first by her daughter and then again at third hand, by the speaker's granddaughter. Mostly, however, since Marjorie does not intervene directly throughout the narrative proper, readers will forget about her framing presence and concentrate on Betty's telling of Lottie's and Lottie's mother's and then her own story. The main narrative ends with Marjorie's birth, and her experience is not presented. Marjorie's framing comments are made when she is forty-seven years old, thus forty-seven years after the central story ends and, as she says in her introduction, shortly after her mother's death. It might be noted that since both Lottie and Betty are dead at the time that Marjorie reproduces their stories, Gibbons here has solved the problems of what might be called postmortem narrative, or deceased narration, which she confronted, perhaps a bit less successfully, with Ruby's narrative in *A Virtuous Woman.*

A central purpose of the narration therefore is the memorializing of Betty, Marjorie's mother, as Marjorie carefully reproduces Betty's responses to her own requests of her mother: "*I would need only say to her, Tell me about your mother and you, and Kentucky and Virginia and the wild way I was born. Tell me about the years that made you*" (3). Betty's responses broaden to include stories of her own grandmother and become her own memorialization of Lottie and the grandmother, as if she cannot tell her own story and her mother's story without including something of her grandmother's story. Marjorie then comments that "*Talking was my mother's life*" (3), introducing a very important theme of the novel and summing up her mother's personality.

Although four women, a four-generation family line, are present, it is the middle two generations, those of Betty and Lottie, who are most important to the plot. The first generation, Bridget's, and the last generation, Marjorie's, are less significant. Bridget's story is briefly told, her early life being summarized and then a trip to Ireland, made as she thinks herself near death, is told in more detail but makes up only a small part of the novel. Marjorie's story as told in the novel consists only of her birth and the fact that at the age of forty-seven she is apparently still single (she gives her last name as Randolph, her mother's married and thus her own birth name) but treasures her family history and the stories of the women who came before her. She remains a shadowy figure.

PLOT AND STRUCTURE

The plot of *A Cure for Dreams* contains the characteristics of oral narrative, not surprising given its narrative method. It is the stringing together of stories, first those told by Lottie to Betty about Lottie's mother and about Lottie herself, then Betty's stories of her own life, concluding with the birth of Betty's child, Marjorie. Their stories are told in a roughly chronological order, except that the story of Bridget's trip to Ireland is not placed where it would belong if it were told as part of Bridget's life before any stories about Lottie. Instead it is told where it belongs in the narratives of Lottie's and Betty's lives, for Betty accompanies Lottie to Kentucky to meet Bridget and then Lottie accompanies Bridget to Ireland. While in Kentucky, Betty learns some information about her father and his family, which had not been told to her by Lottie, thus enlarging somewhat on Lottie's tales as told to her. Stories concerning other characters, especially those of Sade Duplin and Trudy Woodlief, are placed within the narrative, and their placement, as Lottie thought to tell them to Betty, helps to remind readers of the basis in oral storytelling so central to this novel.

In its briefest form, the plot of this novel tells of the coming of Bridget and her family to this country, fleeing from the starvation surrounding them in nineteenth-century Ireland. They settle in rural Kentucky where they scratch out a living. Bridget's daughter Lottie marries young and accompanies her husband to North Carolina. Her husband, a hardworking man, makes a life for them financially but Lottie resists his insistence that she work as hard as he does, and the marriage is not happy. She makes her own life by immersing herself in the lives of the women of the community. Betty, her daughter, accompanies her mother as she wanders about meeting her friends and often arranging the lives of these friends, and the embedded stories come mostly from these experiences. Lottie's husband kills himself, and his loss seems to make little difference in the lives of Lottie and Betty. When Bridget calls, Lottie and Betty travel to Kentucky, where Betty remains, learning about her father's early life and his forebears, while Lottie and Bridget make a trip to Ireland. Bridget had expected to die on this trip but stubborn as ever, she survives, and Lottie brings her back to Kentucky. Like her mother, Betty strikes out from home, but she does it on her own and only briefly. She travels to Richmond to take a secretarial course and then to work. After an ill-fated romance there with a man who turns out to be a drug addict, she returns home and finally marries a man whom she had known from childhood. As the time is now 1941, they marry, and he immediately goes off to the navy. Immediately pregnant, she bears her daughter Marjorie, and the novel proper comes to an end. Readers do learn that Betty's husband returns home safely and, from one or two remarks earlier, may assume that the marriage was a happy one, but both the marriage and the husband are left undeveloped. The story is that of the women, and the men play small parts in the plot.

The plot, told linearly, is a simple one, and readers' interest is maintained by the ways in which its parts are developed. The nesting of narratives, especially Lottie and Betty's, and the details with which the events and relationships are developed are at the heart of the novel's appeal. Additionally, there are several important subplots which enlarge the scope of the story. One which is of particular interest is the story of a woman friend of Lottie's and how she manages to escape from an abusive marriage. Chapter 5 tells the story of Sade Duplin and her unfaithful husband Roy. This subplot is of interest as a compelling story in its own right, but Lottie's participation in Sade's tale helps to characterize her, and additionally the treatment given by Gibbons is a retelling of a well-known literary work which gives the familiar story several new twists.

The source for this subplot is a work from the early twentieth-century tale told twice by Ellen Glaspell, once as a one-act play entitled *Trifles* and once as a short story called "A Jury of Her Peers." Gibbons's retelling, with no overt hints at its source, is faithful in broad outlines and in a number of specific details. In both versions, a country woman, trapped in a loveless marriage, kills her husband. When the killing is investigated, male investigators do not understand the domestic clues to the woman's turbulent state of mind (a kitchen only partly tidied and a quilt with some parts of the stitching uneven), but females present at the scene read the clues, tidy the kitchen, and rip out and correct the stitching. The implication is that the females become accomplices of the murderer because, unlike the male investigators, they understand why she had acted as she had, and they sympathize with her. Tacitly they acquit her, although their goal is to keep her from being accused.

Glaspell's telling of the source story ends there, and readers of the short story or viewers of the play can only conjecture whether the women's actions succeed. Gibbons, however, tells us more. She begins her story at an earlier stage in the wife's experience, giving more information about the marriage than is recounted by Glaspell. She also carries the story further, revealing that Sade not only is not charged with the murder but also that she lives on quite happily and with no apparent suffering from guilt. Nor does her accomplice, Lottie, feel any guilt; indeed, she clearly believes that she has done the right thing for her friend, and that Sade's husband had deserved what he got. (For a fuller and more specific discussion of the relationship between Glaspell's and Gibbons's versions, see Branan [1994].)

CHARACTER DEVELOPMENT

The important characters of *A Cure for Dreams* are all women—the four women of the maternal line whose stories are told and the friends whose stories and experiences also enter into the narrative. Husbands and lovers exist, but they are kept offstage or play minor roles. Several of the women in the novel remain without husbands, and apparently quite happily so. The women of the central family are depicted with varying degrees of fullness, with the first and the last ones being the least well developed. Bridget, the oldest, is seen only in a brief summary of her life and in one episode. She is depicted by Lottie, as related by Betty, and then also to Betty directly through her own experience of her eccentric grandmother. Marjorie, on the other hand, the overall narrator who seems simply to recount what she has been told, appears only in her retelling of what her mother has told her about her birth and then in her framing comments. She thus remains the vaguest and least fully characterized of them all, although her position in the novel is controlling, as all the other narration comes filtered through her.

Bridget O'Cadhain, wife of Sheamus O'Cadhain and the first of these women, is a vivid character and yet one who appears only on the margin. She and her husband come as close to being stereotypes as any characters in the novel: he is a demanding alcoholic, whose commands she defiantly refuses to obey. Her refusal to learn English after she comes to America is symptomatic of her stubborn clinging to familiar ways and her insistence that they are all she needs. Lottie tells us that "The only English thing she ever said that sounded like it was said in her true voice was Jesus, Joseph, Mary Blessed Virgin, Mother of God" (10). These phrases, coming from her Roman Catholicism, are used in frustration, as expressions of anger. She never yields to the wishes or needs of her children, and the irony of her fleeing the potato famine in Ireland and coming all the way to America and then refusing to adapt herself to her new land is clear to her daughter. Violence or the threat of violence simmers close to the surface in their home most of the time. Lottie characterizes Bridget as "the kind of woman who thought nothing of whipping other people's children" (9). Betty believes that Lottie's marriage at the young age of sixteen was a necessary escape from a horrible home environment.

Despite a poor beginning for the family line in the New World because of Bridget's stubbornness and threatened explosive violence, her female descendants are shown as loyal and dutiful. Mothers and daughters are close to each other. Lottie, although she escapes her mother and her home in Kentucky, marrying early and going to North Carolina with her new husband, stays in touch with her family, and when her mother calls, she takes her own daughter back to Kentucky for a visit and accompanies her mother "home" to Ireland. She has her mother's forcefulness, independence, and self-confidence, but she has abilities notably lacking in Bridget. She begins as a romantic, dreaming of a wonderful future husband, but she becomes a practical woman, disillusioned with her own marriage and penetrating in her understanding of other relationships. She cares about others and she listens to them. She reaches out, where Bridget had cared only about herself. Thus she is able to build a community, something completely lacking in her mother's life. Both women are controlling, but Bridget commands others for her own good, whereas Lottie manipulates them for their own sakes. Her destruction of the evidence that would have condemned Sade Duplin to prison for killing her husband is a notable example.

The strong-mindedness in which she resembles Bridget appears over and over. One example nearly has horrible consequences for her own daughter, but in the end it also reveals her ability to listen to others and her nurturing love for her daughter, quite unlike any characteristics of Bridget's. When Betty is twelve, she begins limiting her diet to corn bread and molasses and, in the way of rebellious teenagers, refuses to eat anything else. Lottie tries to tempt her to eat other foods but is not really worried and for some time, despite warnings from her husband, stubbornly will not insist. She assumes that so long as Betty does not go hungry, she is all right. Excusing her, Betty later points out that Lottie did not have the knowledge of nutrition that later would become universal, although at the time Betty's father had argued that the girl needed a more varied diet. Certain that all is well, however, Lottie permits Betty to maintain her odd eating habits until she develops skin problems and fatigue. A doctor does not take Betty's complaints seriously, and so Lottie continues to allow her to restrict her diet until Betty becomes seriously ill. Finally, after her daughter's health is endangered, Lottie insists that the doctor do a thorough job of examining Betty, with the result that he quickly diagnoses pellagra, usually a disease of poor people unable to afford to eat a varied menu, and Betty is soon cured. Lottie, unlike her mother, is able to admit that she had been wrong, but this episode is known in the family as the time Lottie nearly killed Betty (21–25).

Lottie is like her mother in wanting to control her surroundings, but she often does this through manipulation, quite unlike her mother. Because she loves nice clothes and resents her husband's penny-pinching, she persuades him that chintz, organdy, and chiffon (expensive but, to her taste, luxurious fabrics) are actually cheaper than the gingham which really would have suited their pocketbook (16). As she grows up, Betty feels some guilt over this deception (18), but it never seems to bother Lottie, who knows what she wants and goes about getting it in the most practical way she can imagine.

Lottie's honesty is weak in other episodes. When she returns with Betty to Kentucky, she reports that her husband had died a heroic death, rescuing a hobo from in front of a speeding train (82), when actually he had committed suicide from shame and guilt after a young employee is killed in his mill and he behaves with total lack of feeling to his other employees (72–82). Lottie is frank about his death to her daughter and friends, but she refuses to admit the truth to her mother and other relatives in Kentucky. As deeply as Betty loves and admires her mother, she observes how slippery her ethics are but does not comment much on them or evaluate them.

Lottie would never have called herself a feminist, indeed probably would not have known what that meant, but she acts as one. She gathers women about her, molds them into a supportive community, and devises ways for them to survive in their male world. She decides which women are loved by their husbands by the ways in which their husbands speak to them. She puts her powers of observation to work as she tries to see what is good or bad in their marriages (it seems usually to be bad), and then she employs her sharp wits in helping them. She interferes in the lives of others, but always with good motives. Betty speaks of one woman, impoverished and depressed during the depression years, who Lottie "yanked . . . up, brought . . . back to our house, and lent . . . a chintz skirt and her faux ruby barrette" (50). To Betty, Lottie's forcefulness and vigor make her a "walking, talking, free moving picture" (50), and Betty happily spends most of her time with her mother. The mature Betty, telling her stories to Marjorie, sums Lottie up: "On Milk Farm Road she'd remade herself into the Queen Bee, more or less organizing life through knowing everything" (100), hinting at Lottie's forcefulness and vigor, as well as her habit of intruding into other lives and the narrow scope of the world she had made for herself.

The third of these four women, Betty, is the narrator at secondhand of most of the story. Although her telling is filtered through Marjorie, it is Betty's voice that readers hear. She is a loyal daughter, loving her mother and choosing to spend most of her time with her even while observing her eccentricities and commenting upon them. But as her mother had done when she married early, Betty, too, eventually feels the need to leave home and assert her independence. Her journey to Richmond is made comic by her carrying a hatbox (because ladies carried hatboxes when they traveled), which is filled with underclothing because she has no appropriate hat to carry in it. She loses the appearance of sophistication supposed to be given by the hatbox when a fellow passenger insists on seeing the hat inside it, causing her to flee in confusion and embarrassment (117, 119–20). Her mixture of adult dignity and youthful insecurity is amusingly depicted.

She tells her own adventures with zest. She is always generous, and one of first things she describes is buying gifts for the people at home as soon as she begins earning some money by working at a dime store. It is Lottie who recognizes the telltale signs of Stanton's addiction, but once it is pointed out to Betty, she begins to notice other clues and, finally, convinced that he is not a reliable person, she breaks with him. Her courtship by Stanton, her delight in being wooed, and her final rejection of him after she realized he is a drug addict and has been giving pep pills to her, are amusingly recounted and reveal both her lack of knowledge of the world and her good sense and the courage to follow it. Going home to her mother might seem like a surrender of her independence, but that is not in fact completely the case. She soon becomes involved with a young man there, and, as World War II begins, she marries him. But it is at the birth of her daughter that she really establishes her independence from her mother. Polly, the midwife, tells her that "you as much as anybody needs to do this one thing this time without Miss Lottie" (167). Betty's immediate bonding with the baby which she—and Polly—have delivered without the assistance of her dominant mother is a sign that she is now free to begin to build with her own daughter the kind of strong relationship she and Lottie have had.

Marjorie, the last of the central four women, is present only as the child born in the last chapter of the novel proper and as the unobtrusive outside narrator. Except for the interests and affections that may be inferred from the fact of her reproducing her mother's stories, she reveals little of herself. Her brief prologue and epilogue reveal her name and age, and how the book came about (her insistent querying of her mother about the past), as well as the fact that her father came home from the war when she was two years old and that her first memories are of "women talking" (170). Her love for her mother and grandmother and her delight in their stories and in the women's community they depict are easily inferred but are nowhere stated or depicted. She is not given the characterization that the others receive and remains shadowy, even (or perhaps especially) when compared to Bridget, the great-grandmother whom she never knew but about whom she tells as she repeats Betty's stories about her.

Other women characters represent friends of the central women and dramatize the workings of their community. Most prominent among them are Polly Deal, Sade Duplin, and Trudy Woodlief, with Odessa Hightower also worthy of mention. Polly Deal is in some ways a parallel figure to the Mavis of *Ellen Foster* and to Sudie Bee in *A Virtuous Woman*. She is initially introduced by Betty as "a wonderful gingercake-colored woman who worked as our part-time cook and laundress and doubled as a midwife and baby doctor" (29–30). She is a benevolent figure, part of the novel's community of women, who performs necessary functions for Mill Creek Road. She is contrasted with the local doctor, who is not available when needed as Betty is about to deliver Marjorie, but more interesting is her contrast with Odessa Hightower. Odessa is the public health nurse and a less prominent character. Odessa is a voice of rationality and twentieth-century science, insisting on vaccinations and other preventative measures, while Polly holds to some of the superstitions, as well as folk wisdom of the past. Both are depicted favorably, and together they represent the sorts of medical care—from past folkways and contemporary science—available to the women of Milk Farm Road.

Trudy Woodlief is the most prominent of these minor characters in terms of the attention given to her story: four chapters (7, 8, 11, and 12) center around her. She is an outsider to Milk Farm Road, moving there in 1937 with her large family (a husband and several children), and she becomes Betty's close friend. She is a free spirit, who says what she thinks with no thought for how her bluntness will be received. An initial description of her shows her "wearing a very chewed-up-looking robe, with one leg high up on a bureau, smoking a cigarette and shaving her legs with lotion and a straight razor" (56). When her husband, a thief, leaves her and her children, she is pregnant with twins but seems undisturbed by his departure and goes on alone as before. Her children run wild, attending school only occasionally and stealing from everybody (taking odd bits of clothing from clotheslines and so on), but again Trudy is unbothered. Despite her flaws, she is good-hearted, and her ill fortune at being left alone with a large brood of children inspires the women, led by Lottie, to take her under their collective wings. She becomes a part of the community partly because she is generous and open and partly because the women see and respond to her needs. Betty finds her fascinating because of her daring and her unconventionality and feels courageous to have her as a friend.

Sade Duplin's story, already examined in another context, presents another female character whose experiences are also embedded in the text, occupying chapter 5. She is presented as an unhappily married woman who is abused by her husband and seems very weak until, in an act of mutiny against her oppression, she kills him. Like Trudy, she is protected by the women, and, also like Trudy, she is happier and becomes more a part of the broad circle of women after she is husbandless and free.

The male characters of this novel can be briefly considered for none of them are fully characterized. They are significant for their relationship to and treatment of their wives. Bridget's husband, Sheamus O'Cadhain, is notable primarily for shouting commands to his wife and daughter and for demanding that they cater to his most trivial wants. Charles Davies, Lottie's husband, is more fully characterized, but mainly as a sharp businessman who lives to earn money and who is thoughtlessly cruel to his employees and stingy to his wife and daughter. He is also weak, for when his insensitivity to his workers becomes public knowledge, he kills himself. Like other female characters, Lottie remains single when he is gone, and her widowhood is happier than her married life had been, for in it she is able to do as she wishes without having to manipulate her husband. Also very briefly depicted but shown more favorably is Herman Randolph, who courts and marries Betty and then goes off to war, leaving her pregnant. He appears truly to care about Betty, and although his last direct appearance in the novel comes as he is leaving, Marjorie does mention in her epilogue that he had returned safely from the war when she was two, but perhaps it is most revealing that his return is not her earliest memory. He seems to have been a more satisfactory husband than Sheamus or Charles, but his part is very minor. And finally, if Marjorie has had a husband or lovers, no hints are given.

SETTING

As in all Gibbons's novels, setting is basic to plot, characterization, and theme. Here, just as in *Ellen Foster* and *A Virtuous Woman*, the setting is the rural South among people without great means. In *A Cure for Dreams*, the locales are made somewhat more specific than in the earlier novels, as the narration this time comes from somewhat more prosperous and presumably more educated persons. Some place names are given, although they often are quite general. Bridget's origins are in Galway, Ireland, from which she emigrates with her family. Lottie is born and brought up in Bell County, Kentucky, and after her marriage she accompanies her new husband to North Carolina.

As a result, Betty is a native North Carolinian, but she eventually goes off to Richmond, Virginia, for business training and a job. Unlike her foremothers, however, she returns home after an unhappy love affair, and it is in her native area of North Carolina that she finally marries and settles down. Marjorie then is born in North Carolina and presumably is reared there, but readers learn nothing of her history, and although her prologue and epilogue are carefully dated, they are not given any geographic placement.

It is notable that the vaguest of the specified places is the one which is the setting for most of the novel. No county or town name is given, and as in the earlier novels, there is little direct description of the area. People are the center, and place enters in as it relates to the people. It is as if the characters are looking outward from the place they inhabit and which they do not need to describe because they know it so well. What is specific about this North Carolina setting is "Milk Farm Road," which places the action in a neighborhood, not in a town or county. It is the very particular road on which these women live that is essential. It is other places that require specificity because they are different. But even with the other places, the naming of places tends not to become very precise. In fact, the most specific references tying the events of this novel to the South are references to aspects of daily life, such as details about food which are characteristic of the region and of the women's activity of quilting, typical of women's activities in other regions as well.

More precise is the novel's setting in time. Dates are given, making it easy to construct a time line for the lives and some of the events in the novel. Marjorie's prologue and epilogue are dated to December 15, 1989 (1, 171). Lottie and her future husband meet at a Quaker wedding in 1917 (4). At the age of twelve, Betty suffers from pellagra in the summer of 1932 (21). Trudy Woodlief moves to Milk Farm Road in 1937 (55). Lottie's husband's death occurs in 1938 (72), and later that year the trip to Kentucky and Ireland takes place (105). Bridget dies at age ninety-seven (111), but a date is not given for this event, her great age being more important than the actual timing of her going. Betty's courtship with her future husband begins in the fall of 1939 (137). The events of December 7, 1941, leading the United States into World War II and precipitating Betty's swift marriage, are alluded to only as "shortly after this we were bombed" (145), this happening being so momentous as not to need more specific dating. Finally, Marjorie's birth occurs "two days after Thanksgiving of 1942" (162).

These dates mostly refer to important events in the lives of the characters. Other events are more generally placed in time by allusions to historical figures: references to "Mr. Hoover," the president from 1929–1933, place the narrative in the early years of the depression, while mention of "Mr. Roosevelt" moves the time on to the later years of the depression. References to the W.P.A. (the Works Progress Administration, an agency of the Roosevelt depression-era administration which created work for the unemployed) serve the same function. And, finally, there are allusions to "Hitler," for the German dictator is not awarded the respect regularly given the American presidents. All these dates and allusions place *A Cure for Dreams* much more securely in time than were the earlier novels. In fact, the events of this later novel are themselves more dependent on their historical setting than were those of its predecessor.

THEMES

A very important theme of *A Cure for Dreams* is that of talking, of storytelling, of narration. The nested method—through which the story is told, with one speaker (Lottie) quoted by another (Betty) who is then in turn quoted by yet another (Marjorie)—is similar to wooden Russian dolls which are packed one inside another. The complexities of this method call attention to it, as does Marjorie's opening characterization of her mother as one who *"died in a chair talking, chattering like a string-pull doll."* Her comment that *"Talking was my mother's life"* (1) and her closing remark that her own first memories were of *"the sounds of the women talking"* (171) make explicit this emphasis. Gibbons's acknowledgment page includes mention of papers of the Federal Writers Project in the Southern Historical Collection held at the University of Chapel Hill, where she found voices much like those she sought to present in this novel. Her epigraph for the novel is from W.T. Couch, the regional director of the Federal Writers Project, who commented that "With all our talk of democracy it seems not inappropriate to let the people speak for themselves." Like Couch, Gibbons values the authenticity of the lives and voices of women of the period of the generations preceding and including the Great Depression of the 1930s, and where he helped to preserve actual voices, she has in this novel reproduced them in fiction.

All four of the women whose lives are traced in *A Cure for Dreams* live for talking. For all of them, the theme of talking, conversation, language is important, although the way in which it is important varies. Bridget, the first generation, is a speaker of Gaelic in her native Ireland. When she comes to the United States, she refuses to learn English, but she is a forceful and very expressive woman who always manages to make herself clear to others. For Lottie and Betty, talking or conversation is more obviously a central part of daily life. For Marjorie, the youngest, the desires to hear talking and to preserve it are what lead to the existence of the book. She asks her mother for stories, she listens to stories of her mother, grandmother, and great-grandmother, and she reproduces them, in her turn telling them to a wider audience. And she tells them as a whole, linked together by the blood relationships of the women, not just as separate stories, which is how she had received them. For all four women, language and conversation are an important part of living their lives. And for Marjorie, who gives the stories to us, preserving the stories and the language are as important as the listening.

Another important theme in this novel is that of women's solidarity. The use of the embedded narrations implies this theme as it makes Lottie, Betty, and Marjorie sometimes seem to be telling their stories with one voice. They understand each other and they value each other's experiences so much that it is important to them to tell and retell what they learn from each other. The absence of husbands and men in general from much of the narrative is another indication of the importance of this theme. Stories of other women included in the novel also make the same point. The almost complete absence of Trudy's husband is one example. More interesting is Sade's murder of her husband, which is sympathetically presented because the women understand her situation and motivation. Gibbons may have taken the theme of women's solidarity from Glaspell, for it is central in both writers' telling of the murder plot. In Glaspell it appears through the gradual realization of two women of what has happened in the life of the murderess and their unspoken decision to tamper with the evidence. In Gibbons it is made more explicit, as the support for Sade by Lottie and other women of the community in the days after the murder is described.

The story of Jude Duplin is only one example of how the notion of women's solidarity plays out in the novel. The absence of Trudy's husband, present only very briefly, echoes the same notion. The true community here is not town or church but rather women who value and understand each other. Most are married, but the marriages are mostly unsatisfactory. Women who lose their husbands, like Lottie, Sade, or Trudy, remain happily single. Some women, like Polly Deal and Odessa Hightower, are single, and their lack of husbands is not remarked upon. Hints are given that Betty's marriage is happier than most seen in this novel, but like many other men, Betty's Herman remains mostly offstage and there is no extended depiction of the marriage, only the preliminary bridal shower and wedding being presented. The world of *A Cure for Dreams* is a world of women, in which men are present only on the edges. (For another discussion of the themes of women's conversations and their community, see McKee [1997].)

This leads to another theme, one oddly presented partly by its very absence, the theme of marriage. As we have already seen, in the world of this novel, marriage is not a fulfilling part of life for most of these women. Bridget's marriage consists largely of shouted and disobeyed commands, and Lottie's is unsatisfying, as she and her husband have completely different goals and interests. Betty's marriage may have been more successful, but it is not depicted beyond its beginning and a few brief mentions of her husband. Marjorie may never have married, for at the age of forty-seven she is using her birth name and there is no hint of the presence of a husband. Her narrative traces the lives of women who themselves are their family. Marriage is not shown as a way for women to achieve fulfillment. Rather it seems generally to be an oppressive institution for these women.

A CULTURAL READING OF *A CURE FOR DREAMS*

Culture may be broadly defined as the sum total of the characteristics of a particular group (anything from a nation to an ethnic group to the inhabitants of a limited region, even to the employees of a company or the students at a school). These characteristics include beliefs, myths, superstitions, manners, customs, habits, and the like—whatever is generally accepted by the members of the group and influences their behaviors in ways that may differ from the behaviors of members of other groups. Thus, ways of interacting with each other, the music appreciated, the religious beliefs, and many other aspects of daily life may be involved in culture. The word *culture* is sometimes taken to refer to what may better be called *high culture*—classical music and the visual arts, the literature taught in schools, and so on. What is meant here, however, is something quite different, the culture of daily life, not an elitist attitude which evaluates, negatively, some possible aspects of the people's culture in its broadest sense.

Cultural criticism may either apply an understanding of the culture from which an author came, in an attempt to understand why the author's fiction takes the shape it does, or it may seek to analyze the culture depicted in a particular work and thus to understand the nature of the world in which the characters live and the themes which the author is attempting to develop.

All fiction assumes the existence of a culture in which the characters involved in a story are participants. Some science fiction, for example, creates possible cultures of future societies or societies of alien worlds. Historical fiction tries to depict cultures of a past time and place, as well as events of the past. Fiction set in the present uses the author's perception of the culture in which his or her characters move. All of these, and many more, kinds of fiction may use culture in a variety of ways. For example, the culture may merely be used as a background for the action of the story and therefore not become of particular interest to the reader. On the other hand, the author may use the culture as an important strand of the fiction, perhaps to portray some of its characteristics as especially desirable. Or the culture may be shown to be undesirable in some ways, thus being criticized by the author. Yet another possibility is that the author may be simply attempting to portray a particular culture to outsiders, to readers not familiar with it.

In *A Cure for Dreams*, Gibbons has chosen to use as the background of her characters and events the culture of the rural South of the United States in the period covering roughly the first half of the twentieth century. Her more narrow focus, as we have seen, is on the years of the Great Depression of the 1930s and on the lives of women living in that place and that time. In creating the community we have looked at earlier, the women were building their own culture, a culture of solidarity, of caring for and protecting each other. Within that women's culture, they confront and learn to cope with aspects of the broader culture—regional and national—that were crucial to that particular period.

Among the facets of their culture which have not been touched on here previously, several are quite obvious. The insecurity and poverty of the depression, illustrated in the lack of resources of these women and their families, are also illustrated by such historical references to "Mr. Hoover," who seems not to be doing a very good job of helping them achieve the security they wish for, and "Mr. Roosevelt," from whom they seem to hope but not really expect better things. The death of Lottie's husband by suicide following depression caused by his inappropriate behavior after the death of a seventeen-year-old boy in his cotton baler and the social and family condemnation he receives as a result is an indication of the brutality still legally permissible in the period toward employees, as well as of the power of the culture to punish those believed to have broken unspoken social laws. He had not participated in any community solidarity, and he takes his life as a result.

Interesting also is the balancing of ignorance or superstition against newer scientific knowledge which takes some time to filter down to the rural community. One illustration comes in the incident of Betty's suffering from pellagra, a disease understood then by physicians, but not necessarily by ordinary people. And even then, the doctor who first examines Betty does not catch what should be an obvious diagnosis because he makes certain unwarranted and culturally biased assumptions— that pellagra, a disease of nutrient insufficiency, occurs only in the very ignorant, not in relatively middle-class families like Lottie's. Only when Lottie insists, does the doctor examine Betty thoroughly enough to make a proper diagnosis; some might argue that this is an example from the 1930s of the likelihood that women will not be taken seriously by their doctors unless they are very insistent, an insight widely gained only much later.

Another example of a blending of superstition and science comes in the scene in which Betty delivers Marjorie, at home alone with only Polly Deal, a black midwife present to help her. Polly is skillful and loving in assisting Betty, but several interesting things happen after the baby is born. First, Polly puts some drops in the baby's eyes (168). These drops are never explained, but they must be silver nitrate, the use of which in the eyes of newborns in the 1930s and thereafter sharply reduced the incidence of blindness. Polly is up to date in this regard.

Second, Polly hands Betty a "little blue perfume-looking bottle" which she instructs her to blow into in order to be sure that she has expelled all of the afterbirth, or otherwise "whatever afterbirth was left inside would mortify and I would never stop hurting" (168). This appears to be a practice based on superstition.

The third detail is that of the baby's head, soft at birth, being misshapen, going "up in back into sort of a windblister point" which Polly corrects by "shaping" the baby's head with her hands (169–70), again probably a folk practice which has now been superseded by instructions to parents of newborns not to allow their babies to sleep always in the same position.

Finally, Polly writes down the information which will be needed for Marjorie's birth certificate, singing as she does:

> We report births and deaths and all
> When anything is wrong, we the doctor call,
> We hope we never from grace may fall,
> As we go marching on. (169)

The song seems to be a reminder to this unschooled midwife to do all that is legally required as she practices a profession that has often operated outside the law and been scorned by the physicians. Again, we have a blending here of what might be considered the modern with older practices of this particular culture.

6

Charms for the Easy Life
(1993)

Gibbons's fourth novel has features which will be familiar to readers of her previous work. Again it is a first-person narrative, centered around Southern women. Like *A Cure for Dreams*, it traces the experiences of three generations of the women in one family as told by the youngest of them. Here again the Southern setting is basic, but here folkways are more explicitly depicted than in the earlier work. As in the two most recent novels, marriages are described. This novel returns, however, to the single narrator method of *Ellen Foster*. Its events are presented in chronological order, as told by an intelligent and perceptive observer and participant in them. It differs from its predecessors in depicting several important male characters favorably and in presenting successful marriages. Unlike the first two books, it covers the social history of an area as it follows the lives of a family which leaves its rural origins to move to the city. These women also rise in the world, in possessions, in education, and in status. World events, such as the Great Depression and especially the World War II, which impinge on the characters of *A Cure for Dreams*, are much more important in the lives of these women, and indeed tracing their effect is very important to the narrative. Social change is presented along with political events as an important theme. The scope of this novel is therefore broader than that seen in Gibbons's earlier works.

PLOT AND STRUCTURE

The plot of this novel once again is simple: a rural, uneducated midwife marries and with her husband leaves her backcountry home and
moves to a nearby city, a move which is wrong for him but absolutely
right for her. They have a single daughter, and the husband deserts his
wife, who continues her midwifery and gradually learns more and more
about medicine, partly through experience but also through diligent
study of medical texts. She broadens her care for the poor people she
serves until eventually she is practicing medicine without a license. However, she does it so well and so successfully that she is never in any legal
difficulty and, in fact, is able to force the retirement of a legal doctor
because she has observed the effects of his malpractice on several of her
patients. She and her daughter are close, and the daughter's experience
of marriage is no better than her own had been. Her husband is a "cad,"
according to his own daughter, and no one mourns his death. This third-
generation daughter is brought up in a household of women: her grandmother, her mother, and herself. The three are very different from each
other, but all are very close.

As the plot unfolds, the grandmother becomes more and more prominent and respected, the mother becomes lonely and finally finds a new
lover who is far finer than her husband had been, and the granddaughter
grows up a happy but shy, gifted, and wise young woman who eventually finds her own love with the son of a prominent and wealthy family. Told bluntly, the novel sounds like a romantic saga, and there
certainly are elements of romance in it; the daughter's love affair is particularly criticized by a few reviewers as sentimental and too good to be
true. But it is also grimly realistic in parts. These women progress from
rural poverty to urban comfort, from a world of racism, bigotry, and
ignorance to a place where they can support tolerance and understanding, and where their love of books of all kinds does not seem outlandish.
They see much suffering along the way, and they do what they can to
lessen it. But they bring with them some rural folkways and customs,
and they never forget their origins. The improvement in their world
parallels the improvement in their own situation. The story closes with
the grandmother's death, which comes immediately after a day in which
her great achievements have been recognized, and with the happy acceptance of her granddaughter into her fiancé's family.

There might be some argument over exactly which character is the
protagonist, the grandmother or the granddaughter. Both are more fully

characterized, in differing ways, than the woman in the middle generation, the grandmother because she is a stronger and more interesting character and the granddaughter because she depicts her own feelings and interpretations through her narration. Her narrative begins with events and people she never knew—her grandmother's early years, the family's migration to the city, and her mother's life before her own birth. Like Marjorie in *A Cure for Dreams*, the similarly named Margaret of *Charms for the Easy Life* recounts stories that have been told to her, but unlike Marjorie the greater part of her narrative concerns events she has lived through and which she tells from her own observation. She might be thought of as protagonist because of her presence as narrator and because of the gradual shift in the story's emphasis from the concerns of her grandmother and mother to her own life as her narrative becomes about herself instead of about herself in relation with the others. Much of the later part of the plot deals with her experiences as a hospital aide during World War II and with her courtship and engagement.

However, arguments for considering the grandmother the protagonist are at least equally strong. She is the only one of the three central characters to be present throughout the novel, which opens with a statement about work and closes with her death. In addition, she is the strongest and the most interesting of the characters, and it is she who lives through great changes in the rural South in the twentieth century. Like Gibbons's women in *A Cure for Dreams*, she is a powerful personality, self-assured to the point of arrogance, but she is also empathetic and involves herself in people's lives for their well-being, not for her own pleasure.

The novel's structure may also be indicating that Margaret is the true protagonist, the true center of interest in the novel, and that the grandmother, like the mother and a number of other characters, is important principally for what she teaches Margaret; the examples set by all the characters help her to become a mature and strong young woman. Chronological in its presentation and covering directly the period of a little over thirty years from 1910, when the grandmother leaves her rural home with her husband and six-year-old daughter, to a Christmas celebration in 1942, Margaret's narration moves quickly through the earliest parts of her story, which may seem like a catalog of suicides and which of course she describes as they have been told to her. Her birth (in 1924) occurs in the second of the novel's unnumbered sections (there are sixteen in all), and by the beginning of the third section, the narrative has progressed to 1936 as Margaret is now describing events and people from firsthand knowledge. From the sixth section, which occurs in 1940, the pace of the story slows, and the last eight sections trace events through 1942, concluding after Christmas.

NARRATIVE METHOD

As narrator, Margaret stands at the center of the story's presentation to readers. She moves from describing events and people at early stages of their lives, before she was around to "know" them, to when the narrative reaches her own life and events and people she actually remembers. She then begins to describe most things as she observed them, and her narrative slows and becomes more detailed. She tries to be an objective and accurate teller of the tale, and one mark of her aim in this regard, as well as of her imagination and creativity, is shown in the things she wants to tell but which she does not actually know from her own knowledge. When she presents information which she would have no way of knowing, she is careful to state that such material is her own reconstruction of what must have happened or of what a character must have been thinking or feeling. One important example of such a reconstruction, here actually more of a conjecture, comes as she is describing her grandparents' brief reunion after years of separation and then their immediate renewed separation and her grandfather's death. Margaret tries to understand why her grandmother had seemed to run to him with ardent love and wonders whether she was sincere in running to him or whether she had already been plotting revenge for his long desertion. Notice the verbs in the following passage:

> Love *seemed* to be screaming out as she ran, or maybe, since love and revenge grow from the same kernel of want, I was mistaken. She *could've* been hoarding a dream of vengeance for more than twenty years, and that run was part of the plan. Or the run *may have been* true, and the reality of starting her life over with a stinking, old, untrustworthy man hit her as she watched him gum his food. . . . She may have looked at him sleeping and despised him for leaving her. . . . I wondered what they said to each other . . . what they did for each other until that moment when my grandmother decided the man had had use of her heart long enough. (77; italics added)

Clearly Charlie Kate did not discuss her very private feelings with Margaret, and Margaret is left to wonder—and to relate her guesses as to her grandmother's motivation. This passage is typical of a number of points within the narrative at which Margaret presents more context or explanation for events or actions than she actually knows. But her reliability as narrator is enhanced by the care with which she identifies those explanations as her own imagining.

A very bright and widely read person, Margaret presents her narrative in smooth and effective prose. Unlike Gibbons's earlier narrators, her grammar and spelling are impeccable. She uses a variety of sentence constructions and a wide-ranging vocabulary, filled with literary allusions, many of them references to books she and her mother and grandmother were reading and discussing with each other. Because of her education and interest in learning, the narrative of this novel is much more firmly and specifically situated in its time and place than were the earlier books. Margaret, and indeed her older family members, are very concerned with the wider world around them, not like Gibbons's earlier characters who were fixed in their own experience and looking mainly to their own immediate surroundings and community. All this is clearly conveyed by Margaret's narrative.

CHARACTER DEVELOPMENT

As might be expected from Gibbons's earlier novels, the women here are not only the center of interest, but also they are strong, self-willed characters who know what they want and find ways to go about getting it. The three of them, Charlie Kate, Sophia, and Margaret, are so close and so much a unit that it is difficult to discuss their characterizations separately. Gibbons's own reluctant explanation of the novel's subject is that "it's about three women . . . and what they give to and take from each other" (Summer 1993, 60). The strongest of them is the grandmother, a powerful personality. She is officially named "Clarissa Kate" but always insists on being called "Charlie Kate." Margaret suggests that she probably considered her official name "spineless" (2), but it is also notable that the name she rejects is traditionally feminine whereas the one she prefers contains both masculine and feminine elements, quite appropriate for this self-assured woman who makes a place for herself, quite illegally, in a male profession. The first detail given by Margaret about her, in fact, is that by the age of twenty she was already "an excellent midwife" (1). Few details of her earliest years are given, only that she claimed to have had a "wild-animal sort of babyhood," that her "parents kept sheep" (3). Her marriage to a river ferryman in 1902 and the birth of her daughter in 1904 are quickly described, although the childbirth, with its accompanying folklore aspects (smelling red pepper blown through the end of a freshly picked peacock quill in order to make her sneeze and hasten the birth [3]), is briefly recounted.

For Charlie Kate, the most important things in life are her medical work and her family, consisting of her daughter and granddaughter. She apparently never really regrets the loss of her husband, who deserts her and her daughter because he yearns for the river life they had left. When he returns years later, she goes back to him briefly but abandons him almost immediately to return to her daughter and granddaughter, and she lives the rest of her full and productive life in happy singleness.

She is as self-assured in her medical work as in her family life. At the beginning, she relies on her skills in delivering babies and on her knowledge of herbs and folk remedies. But she reads widely, in literature but also in medical journals, and she soon is performing minor—and even major—surgeries in kitchens and wherever her patients are for people who otherwise would not have medical care. As her reputation grows, she is permitted to prescribe medications, all quite illegally but with the support of a few prominent medical men who see her successes and realize the value of her work to the community.

When she first settles in Raleigh with her husband, she lives in the mill district, an area inhabited by poor white people who lack the most basic modern conveniences. Appalled at the lack of sanitation, she manages to have sewers brought into the area, and she gives lessons in the use of flush toilets where needed (9). Public health is a major concern of hers, and she becomes known beyond Beale Street by her work in this area, as well as by her treatment of the patients who throng to her for care.

Her treatment of patients is somewhat idiosyncratic. For example, she uses anesthetics (chloroform obtained by mail order from a veterinary supply firm) for women, but not for men, when she performs dental procedures, because she "believed that although women, as a rule, could stand more pain and take more punishment than men, they should not have to and would not ever suffer under her care" (10–11). In later years, she even anticipates the much heralded treatment for polio victims developed and publicized by the Australian nurse, Sister Kenny (213–14).

Through her working life she develops from a little-trained midwife who relies heavily on folk remedies to a skilled medical practitioner who, despite her lack of any formal training or education, is highly regarded by the real physicians in her community for her competence as a healer and for her effective attempts to improve public health, especially that of those who are poor and those who are black. At the end of her life, she is easily being referred to as "Dr. Birch," although of course she has absolutely no right to that title. At the end of the novel, she experiences a day of triumph at a party given by the wealthy and prominent parent of Margaret's new fiancé where she is repeatedly recognized and honored as a leading physician and citizen of the city. That she is deeply moved by this recognition is indicated by her uncharacteristic self-deprecation to Margaret after it is over: "Think of the living I could make removing warts door to door" (287). It is fitting that her death follows immediately upon this moment of success, and the novel closes with Margaret's finding her and honoring her in the way Charlie Kate had taught her to recognize death.

Charlie Kate's daughter (and Margaret's mother), Sophia, is quite different from both her mother and her daughter, who become especially close to each other. She is more conventional, more concerned with her appearance, more in need of a man in her life. Like her mother, she is deceived by romantic illusions when she marries for love, and like her mother's, her marriage starts out well but ends unhappily as she, like her mother, is deserted. She learns that he had been flagrantly unfaithful to her (repeating her own father's treatment of Charlie Kate). Unlike her mother, Sophia does not find fulfillment in work, and widowhood for her is a state of loneliness which she wishes to end. As strong-willed as her mother, when a marriageable young woman, she had refused to have anything to do with Charles Nutter, her mother's young protégé, an attractive and bright young man whose later success proves that Charlie Kate had been right in singling him out as someone special. Instead she had chosen a man whom her (and his) own daughter describes simply as a "cad." She tends, as this suggests, to act on impulse and to live by feelings, but like her mother and her daughter, she is bright and efficient when she cares to be.

Margaret describes her young mother as sometimes having a "petulant childlike beauty" (26), stubborn, romantic, and idealistic, but able to work hard and effectively when necessary. She lacks the ambition for medicine which is basic to both her mother and daughter, and where her mother's reading varies from classic literature to medical texts and journals, Sophia's includes classic literature but also such romantic volumes as *Gone with the Wind*, which Charlie Kate and Margaret scorn. In general, then, she is presented as a less serious, less intense, less committed, and more self-involved person than is either her mother or her daughter. This does not make her an unlikable character, however, for she is good-hearted and loving, and both Charlie Kate and Margaret are glad for her when she finds a new—and better—man in Richard Baines.

Margaret presents herself as a shy but very bright girl who doesn't quite fit in among other young people, is not interested in boys, and lives to read and to accompany her grandmother on her medical rounds. She is formed by her grandmother and her mother, scorning her father and seeming, in retrospect, to be glad when he left them. It is significant that she has her first menstrual period in the week of her father's death (42), becoming a young woman at the time her family becomes purely female. From childhood she seems to be preparing for the work of a doctor, and her grandmother seems to be training her for that profession, preparing Margaret to achieve the skill and knowledge she has and the credentials she lacks. Despite her shyness and feelings of being different, of not belonging, Margaret is a self-sufficient and self-assured person. She doesn't really mind being an outsider, and when she finally has a disastrous blind date with a smug Yale man, she sees him for the arrogant snob he is. She recognizes the qualities of the young soldier who is to become her fiancé, being drawn to him by their mutual interests and admiration of each other's vitality and character. Well trained by her grandmother, she is a better judge of young men than her mother.

Her ability to judge people perceptively and quickly is notable. The contrast between her reactions to the Yale man and Tom Hawkings is particularly notable here. Her characterization of the father who left her family when she was twelve as a cad is another example. She does not even give names for the men whose characters she scorns. Neither her father nor her grandfather is named; that her grandfather's last name is Birch becomes apparent only from the fact that Birch is the birth surname of her mother (Sophia Snow Birch [2]), as well as the last name of her grandmother (called Dr. Birch in her last days [203]). Even the Yale man with whom she has a blind date remains nameless. In contrast, the name of Tom Hawkings III is given as he is first introduced (195), and Charles Nutter, the protégé of Charlie Kate and eventually a leading physician, is also named when first mentioned (21). Sophia's suitor is introduced as Mr. Richard Baines (93) and called Mr. Baines by Charlie Kate for a long time, as she, like Margaret, has doubts of him as well as by Margaret in her narration. Eventually, as he finally marries Sophia, they relent and call him Richard. That Margaret has greater sympathies for women is indicated by the fact that throughout the novel, female characters are given names; it is only the males whose evaluations are shown by the ways in which she refers to them.

An enthusiastic and loving young woman, Margaret is close to both her mother and her grandmother. In fact, the three of them are often inseparable, especially after the desertion of Margaret's father (Charlie Kate had been so angered by that marriage that she refused to visit their home until after he is gone, at which point she moves in with Sophia and Margaret). The two younger women accompany Charlie Kate on her medical rounds and assist her with various procedures, although Margaret is the better helper. They read and discuss all sorts of literary works and occasionally go to movies together. Margaret's taste is formed by these experiences, although she comes to agree more with her grandmother than with her mother's more sentimental inclinations. She seems happy to follow the life path her grandmother has laid out for her: college and a medical degree, followed by a practice of her own. In the first years of World War II, she, along with her mother and grandmother, becomes involved in volunteer war work, Sophia principally as a Red Cross Volunteer but Charlie Kate and Margaret in a veterans' hospital to which they are introduced by Dr. Charles Nutter. Charlie Kate is officially acting as a nurse but is actually performing as a physician, while Margaret reads letters to and writes replies for seriously wounded men. Margaret has some heart-wrenching experiences doing this, cruelly reading a "dear John" letter to a blinded man before she realizes what it is. At the urging of her grandmother, she several times revises extensively letters these men dictate to her, from generous motives but occasionally getting into trouble as a result. It is through this work that she meets Tom Hawkings. Charlie Kate implies to Margaret that she has a future with Tom, instructing her to make plain to him that she intends to get an education, fulfilling her own professional dreams, before having children. She is to have a marriage of equals, not a traditional union in which she would be subordinated to her husband.

Charlie Kate's prediction for Margaret and Tom seems to be beginning to come true as the novel ends, for they are engaged, to the great delight of both families. Margaret shares the novel's final emphasis with her grandmother—one appropriate but sad ending and one happy ending—as she is joyfully looking forward to her future life with Tom but also beginning to grieve for her dead grandmother. She follows the folk death rituals Charlie Kate had taught her, finding comfort in them.

Gibbons's final words, then, look to the past, that is, a rich life by a woman from another time and other ways, and to the future, a productive and happy life as expected by modern young women. But the two are oddly one, for Margaret's life will be an improved variation on the example set her by Charlie Kate. Where Charlie Kate had an unsuccessful marriage with a weak man and was a completely self-made person, Margaret will have a happy marriage with an understanding and loving husband, and she will have the professional training and credentials her grandmother lacked. In essentials, however, Margaret will follow Charlie Kate's lead, for she has her grandmother's ethics and sensitivity, her concern for those who are poor and downtrodden, and her service to her community will surely be for her day a parallel to that which Charlie Kate's was in hers.

The three women are so central to the novel that it is unnecessary to go into much detail about others. Among significant characters who are discussed in other connections are Louise and Dr. Charles Nutter, the protégé of Charlie Kate and leading physician, and his wife, who together model the possibility of happy marriage between two equals who love each other and their work and make an effective team. Mr. Richard Baines, Sophia's suitor and eventual husband, and Tom Hawkings, who becomes Margaret's fiancé, are also good men, who recognize the qualities of the eccentric family of women into which they marry, and who contrast with the weak and nameless men who had earlier married, betrayed, and left Charlie Kate and Sophia. But all these characters, and others, play secondary roles to the three women, and indeed the male characters have been criticized as being less effectively and fully drawn than the females. Perhaps, given the central subject of the novel, this discrepancy is inescapable.

THEMES

A theme in *Charms for the Easy Life*, which is of particular interest for readers of Gibbons's earlier novels, is that of marriage, for this novel—like the others—shows several failed marriages but nevertheless offers a more balanced picture. It is true that both Charlie Kate and Sophia's marriages end badly, but each of these women has some joy from her marriage. Both marry for love, perhaps a somewhat romantic and unrealistic view of love, but nevertheless each does care for her husband and each man seems to care about his wife. It is just that one, Charlie Kate's husband, finds himself unable to live in the urban setting which turns out to be essential for her, and the second, Sophia's husband, finds himself unable to be faithful to her. Neither woman is ultimately able to forgive her husband's lapses—Charlie Kate the desertion and then the repeated infidelity of her husband and Sophia the flagrant unfaithfulness of hers. Writing in an unusually judgmental way, Margaret repeatedly refers to her father, whom she remembers well since he is with the family until she is twelve, as a "cad," but she recounts her information about her grandfather, whom she never knows although he reappears after her father's death, with more sympathy. At least, she shows empathy for his longing for the river he had to leave when they moved to the city, the longing which she believes caused his desertion. She does, however, point out that the single lesson which Sophia learned from her mother's experience is, "A man will leave you" (14), a lesson which is proved accurate in her own married life. Charlie Kate remains happily single after her husband's departure, but Sophia, who is a more conventionally feminine woman, suffers from great loneliness. For Charlie Kate, a husband turns out to be an unnecessary encumbrance, but for Sophia, a husband is necessary for fulfillment.

Other marriages and potential marriages indicate that the institution is not always destructive. Dr. and Mrs. Nutter and the adult Hawkings model two couples who have interests in common and who work well together. Louise Nutter and Mrs. Hawkings are both women who are assertive and who have their own interests and concerns, not women who have submerged their own identities in their husbands, although it would have been easy for them to do so as both men are successful and indeed powerful in their communities. The marriages which succeed in this novel are those between equals who enjoy each other and are able to let each other be themselves. This is the kind of marriage that seems to lie ahead for Margaret at the end of the novel, for Tom and Margaret are initially attracted to each other by their mutual interests and abilities to banter with each other, as well as by physical attraction. Perhaps more problematical will be the marriage of Sophia and Richard Baines, although they have certainly known each other long enough to be certain of their decision, and they do love each other. But there is still a bit of a romantic attitude in Sophia's approach to the marriage, and it is also clear that she needs the marriage to allay her loneliness. Margaret, it seems clear, has all the resources and the abilities which could enable her to build a life as a doctor, much like a more modern version of the grandmother who has been largely responsible for her values and goals. Sophia, on the other hand, lacks the kind of independent spirit that both Charlie Kate and Margaret have in abundance, and this quality, the novel suggests, helps to enable a couple to build a happy marriage.

Another theme of interest is that of reading and education. The women of this novel are all constant readers, and the text is sprinkled with allusions to the books and authors they read and discuss with each other. These range from medical texts and journals (especially Charlie Kate, of course, who uses some of these to read a small Margaret to sleep with [39]), to such authors as Dickens, Thoreau, Hawthorne, Twain, Wharton, and Flaubert. They are up-to-date in their reading, for among the works mentioned are *To Have and Have Not* (published in 1937) by Hemingway, *The Grapes of Wrath* (1939) by Steinbeck, and such current (in 1940) authors as Marjorie Kinnan Rawlings, James Thurber, Eudora Welty, and William Faulkner. The Faulkner references are particularly interesting, for he had not yet achieved a high reputation in this period and in fact was generally reviewed unfavorably, but Margaret is particularly fond of his work and uses an ability to appreciate his work as a kind of touchstone in evaluating some of the people she meets. Another interesting allusion relates to *Gone with the Wind*, the film and not the book, which the three women go to see. Charlie Kate expects to hate the film, and she and Margaret walk out on it very quickly, scorning it, presumably for its romantic version of the old South. The romantic and feminine Sophia, however, remains to see it through and as a result meets Richard Baines, who is to become her second husband. The frequent use of literary allusions differentiates this novel from the three which preceded it, and their presence helps to characterize the highly intelligent and bookish women of this family.

Two other themes, both of which illustrate the grounding of this novel in the American South in the early twentieth century, are the appearance of racism in the post–Civil War and pre–World War II American South and the uses of folkways in the Southern culture of the period. The former appears primarily in several incidents, while the second is prominent throughout the entire novel, in both important episodes and in passing references.

From almost the beginning of this story, it is clear that Gibbons's characters are out of step with the mainstream of their society in many ways, not the least their attitudes toward race relations. A striking episode sets the tone here. As Charlie Kate and her husband are making their way to the place where they will now live, Margaret says simply, "Something happened." The something, introduced in this understated, almost off-hand, way, is the aftermath of a lynching. Charlie Kate and her husband find the man hanging but still alive, and they cut him down and are able to revive him. The man rides with them to Wake County, and announces that he is now safe from any pursuit, because people will find him missing and believe that it was Jesus who rescued him and that he now has "the power of God" in him (6). The brevity with which this incident is told and the matter-of-fact way in which it is presented and seems to be received by both Charlie Kate and the lynching victim himself suggest how nearly normal such events were in that time and place. But Charlie Kate's (and her husband's) rescue of the man and their transporting him, as an equal, along with them also reveals her rejection of this racism. The novel's ironic title comes from this episode, for the lynched man presents Charlie Kate and her husband with a good luck piece which he calls an "easy-life charm" and describes as "the hind foot of a white graveyard rabbit caught at midnight, under the full moon, by a cross-eyed Negro woman who had been married seven times" (6), an example of the folklore and regional superstition that play an important role in this novel. The charm, incidentally, seems to be forgotten until at the end of the novel Margaret, at Charlie Kate's urging, gives it to Tom as a particularly valuable artifact. . . . At this time it has transcended its origin in a racist episode and become a family treasure, but it has failed to bring anyone, not the lynching victim and not Charlie Kate, the promised "easy life."

Other examples of racism are also important, most markedly in the early years. One striking description illustrates classism as well but reveals how much more deeply ingrained discrimination is against those who are both poor and black than against those who are poor and white. The neighborhood into which Charlie Kate moves when she first comes to the city is a poor white neighborhood which lacks such elementary things as paving and a sewage system. She is able to persuade the textile mill owner of the area to put in boardwalks in several particularly muddy places by appealing to his conscience. Modern plumbing presented more of a problem, but she does finally succeed in getting sewage lines laid. Of course, as she later told Margaret, the race of the inhabitants should not have made any difference at all, but knowledge that the politicians might have some concern about poor white although not about poor black people gave her a tactic to use in accomplishing the action needed. In this case, she uses the ingrained racism of the city fathers to overcome their class prejudices.

Charlie Kate and her descendants are color blind. Charlie Kate cares for black and white patients and is appalled at the double standard she sees in the treatment given by some members of the medical establishment. One black woman dies after a white doctor has not taken her complaints seriously, assuming that because she is both old and black, she must simply be suffering the intestinal results of a poor diet. The woman, of course, has cancer, as Charlie Kate recognizes and, because of his lack of concern, dies a possibly unnecessary death. Charlie Kate cares tenderly for her until that death occurs, in striking contrast to her credentialed colleague, and her anger leads her to take action. By this time having achieved some recognition and respect, she is able to go to see to it that the negligent and biased doctor is forced to retire early. Charlie Kate always acts on her principles, and the novel, through her, illustrates some of the effects of the unthinking distinction between the races so long taken for granted in the American South.

One last brief example occurs years later. The three women and Mr. Baines see a man drowning and rescue him, Charlie Kate then gives him mouth-to-mouth resuscitation, while two women passersby stop and observe as if seeing some sort of tourist attraction. The women, unconcerned, walk on after the excitement seems to be over, while Charlie Kate and the others see to it that the old man gets home to his family. Only then is it indicated, as an almost irrelevant afterthought revealed through details mentioned for other reasons, that the old man is black (a member of an A.M.E. Zionist church, a predominantly black denomination) and that there might have been danger to him and them from the Ku Klux Klan as a result of this episode had she not been the midwife for the mother of a local Klan leader (183–84).

Folklore and folkways make up an important theme in *Charms for the Easy Life*. The use of one such folklore element, a charm, to give the novel its title has already been mentioned, as has the importance to Charlie Kate's medical practice of her knowledge of herbs and folk cures. She herself explains the line which she refuses to cross, that between natural medicine and black magic, although as Margaret recognizes, she encourages her patients to allow more conventional treatment by also using the folk methods they were familiar with and trusted. It is notable that the proportion of superstition to scientific medical skill in Charlie Kate's practice goes down as the novel proceeds and time passes.

A number of folk beliefs are sprinkled throughout the text, adding to that sense of real grounding in a specific time and place which is so strong in the book. One striking example is that of the mad hermit, afflicted by a terrible boil on his neck, which he tries, unsuccessfully, to cut off. Before Charlie Kate is able to help him, he would stand in the middle of the road, flagging down cars, and asking about "his charms," items with magical powers. In addition to calling for his "charms," he tries a number of folk cures, using such "medicines" as urine, the tail of a black cat, an albino's used handkerchief, and raw onion. The listing of folk charms and cures using them goes on for around three-quarters of a page, but all fail, and finally he seeks help from Charlie Kate, who is able to solve his problem without the use of magic (115–18). This episode reveals characteristic behavior on the part of the three main women of the novel: Charlie Kate acts with her usual medical skill, Sophia is useless and finally passes out, while Margaret watches with interest and assists her grandmother.

A particularly interesting folk custom, a system of death rituals, is presented several times, in fact finally helping to increase the emotional impact of the novel's conclusion. These rites include covering windows and mirrors and stopping clocks in a house as soon as an inhabitant dies, and they are presented and explained in the third chapter, which might be called a "death chapter," for in it three deaths occur. It is the death of Margaret's father which causes Charlie Kate to follow this old folk custom. She explains that she is following tradition—her mother and grandmother and preceding generations of women had followed these ways, and so, even though she knows her actions have no magic power, she carries on the old practice. After the death by cancer, untreated by a racist physician, of Maveen, a black woman, Charlie Kate again performs this old ritual (89). And finally—and fittingly, as a final act of love—Margaret performs these rites, which her grandmother had taught her, for Charlie Kate herself (289).

Often associated with these death rituals is the folk belief that if a person dies leaving important things unsaid that person will "purge," die with a bit of foam at the mouth. Charlie Kate seems to give this belief some credence, for upon learning of her estranged husband's death, she asks if he had purged (79–80). Apparently she is pleased to be told that he had, for this might mean he wished to tell her he was sorry for his treatment of her. That the deaths of both Maveen and Charlie Kate are peaceful is indicated to Margaret by the fact that neither had purged (89, 289), and Margaret is following the teachings of Charlie Kate in checking to see whether either of them has done so. In performing the death rituals and in observing whether a dying person has purged, Margaret follows the custom of her grandmother and foremothers further back, as Charlie Kate had done and as she had taught Margaret to do. This following of folk customs in which she doesn't really believe is the last homage Margaret can pay to the grandmother she so dearly loves.

SETTING

Like Gibbons's earlier novels, *Charms for the Easy Life* is set in the American South, largely among poor and ignorant people. Unlike the other books, however, the central characters are widely read and knowledgeable about the world beyond their immediate horizons. As a result, setting, both in time and place, is clearly indicated. Exact place names and precise times are given, particularly after Charlie Kate leaves the rural river surroundings of her origins. From then on, the setting is Raleigh, North Carolina, and its surroundings, and the dates of most of the action are 1936 and then 1940 through Christmas of 1942. Gibbons is always more concerned with her characters and their actions than she is with descriptions of place, allowing what the people are like, how they behave, and what they believe, to create a sense of place. Nevertheless, in this novel there are comments about both the poor mill district in which Charlie Kate and her family live when they first come to Raleigh and the wealthy neighborhoods in which the powerful members of society live, including finally the family into which Margaret will marry. In one notable scene, Sophia sums up the difference between these two sorts of environments, for that contrast is more important in Gibbons's narrative than is the actual appearance of either sort of place. When Charlie Kate enters a wealthy household, Sophia finds it remarkable that while other people who live very near go hungry, they have the luxury of a butler.

Gibbons generally gives her greatest descriptive attention to the details of interiors in which action occurs. For example, details evoking the charms the hermit had used in trying to operate on his boil are sharply indicated and help the reader understand why Sophia faints, as well as add to admiration for Margaret and Charlie Kate, who do not. The Christmas dance at the veteran's hospital evokes its special time in history with descriptions of the playing of songs by Benny Goodman, Nelson Eddy, and Johnny Mercer (212), of a "clot of young men" hanging around the few attractive young women there (215), and of the gold-digging, camp-following "Allotment Annies" (218), so called because they hoped to marry soldiers in order to receive the allotments from soldiers' paychecks automatically sent to their wives during World War II.

Gibbons's sharp eye for detail enables her to re-create a time and place economically, without obtrusive set pieces of description.

A FEMINIST READING OF *CHARMS FOR THE EASY LIFE*

The feminism of *Charms for the Easy Life* must be evident to even a casual reader (see chapter 4). Centering around three strong women of a single family who create their own place in the world, it exemplifies the strain of feminist literature which creates role models for women readers. These women never feel inferior to men; indeed, they mostly reveal that they are superior. However, each of the three women dramatizes a different possibility for women in the American South—a rebel, a more conventional woman, and finally a woman who combines the best of the other two.

Charlie Kate, the oldest and the fullest example here of a truly strong woman who makes her own life, comes from impoverished surroundings and from a culture of ignorance and superstition. Beginning as a midwife and thus by definition primarily devoted to delivering babies and serving poor women who do not have scientific medical care available, she manages by her own hard work and study to make herself equal to and even better than fully trained and highly respected physicians.

She recognizes and nurtures talent, encouraging first a young man (whom she first hopes will marry Sophia, only to have that hope disappointed by her daughter's poor initial taste in men) and then, closer to her heart, her granddaughter. Her world always extends far beyond her own household, thus giving an example of an unconventional woman who refuses to be restricted to the socially acceptable focus on home and family. From the beginning, even when she is romantically in love with her unworthy husband, she is working outside her home. And she makes a difference in her society from the very beginning. She observes injustice and acts upon it, seeing to the installation of sidewalks and sewers in a poor white neighborhood and giving medical care and nurturing to blacks and whites with no distinctions between them. She has no concern for her appearance, and once her husband has betrayed her, she feels no need for a man in her life.

Sophia, from the middle generation, lacks the courage and unconventionality of her mother. A sympathetic character like the others, she is the most bound to the assumptions of her time and place, a kind of opposite to her mother in some respects. She is pretty and very concerned about her appearance and dress. When her marriage ends, as her mother's had, she grieves and suffers deep loneliness, as her mother had not. Unlike her mother, she longs for a new relationship, and she is successful in achieving one. Like her mother and daughter, she is an avid reader, and in many respects her taste is as good and her interests are as broad as theirs, for the three of them read and discuss with each other many great writers. But there is always an edge of conventionality to her, as is shown in her reading by her fondness for such sentimental and stereotyping popular fiction as *Gone with the Wind*, which Charlie Kate and Margaret scorn. Sophia never has the strength of character to develop the individuality and courage that her mother has in abundance, and thus she—unlike the others—does not serve as a feminist role model.

Margaret, the member of the third and youngest generation, combines some of the most marked characteristics of the older two. She has her grandmother's drive and love of healing, and she has Charlie Kate's independence. Shy and never a member of the in-group in school, she is content to go her own way. Although she resists going away to college because this will mean leaving her mother and grandmother, she does not seem to feel any pressure to conform to the ways of her peers. The lack of success of her one blind date does not particularly bother her, and she makes plans for college and a medical career, not for marriage and motherhood. Nevertheless, she is concerned about her appearance and dress, having taken on some of her mother's more conventionally feminine traits. When she meets Tom Hawkings, she does not go out of her way to attract or flatter him, instead attracting him by her very naturalness and qualities of intelligence and spunk. Uniting many qualities of her grandmother and mother, she seems bound for a life which will manage to combine the professionalism and skill of Charlie Kate with the care for husband and family desired by Sophia and the social consciousness of both older women. Both mother and grandmother's dreams for themselves, largely separately fulfilled in their own experiences, seem bound to be successfully fulfilled in Margaret's life. The novel thus has presented several possibilities for women's lives, finally bringing about a resolution in which a combination of work and love is possible.

7

Sights Unseen
(1995)

Gibbons's fifth novel, *Sights Unseen*, is, like her first, *Ellen Foster*, drawn from her own experience. The novel's substance is a child's observations of her mother's incapacity from mental illness and its effect upon her. The family, however, is quite different from that of Ellen Foster, and all characters—father, grandparent, uncle, and aunt—are quite different from their parallels in the earlier book. Thus it stands as a completely independent work of fiction, and no reader who was not acquainted with some of the facts of Gibbons's biography would be apt to assume that both works took their inspiration from the author's life. The illness is the manic-depression which affected her mother as well as herself. Whereas Ellen's mother killed herself, as had Gibbons's mother, the adult in this new novel receives medical treatment and is returned healthy to her family.

In technique and theme, *Sights Unseen* bears some of the usual earmarks of its author's other fiction. A first-person narrative is once again used, the style is suffused with humor, and the overall tone is optimistic despite some very painful subject matter. As before, female characters are at the center of the novel's action and meanings. The setting of the American South, with little direct attention to landscape but important use of customs, language, and issues of race and class, is again notable. This novel, like its predecessors, is short, but like them it is rich in meanings, in emotion, and in theme.

PLOT, NARRATIVE METHOD, AND STRUCTURE

The plot of *Sights Unseen* may be summed up briefly: young girl observes and describes her mother's insanity, treatment, recovery, and subsequent life as a rational and normal woman. However, there is much more to it than this, for the impact on the family, not just the girl, is clearly depicted, individual events and indeed periods within the mother's life are detailed, and the effects of the insanity upon family members, as well as their attempts to cope with it, are significant parts of the story. Complexity is added by the narrative method and by the novel's structure, which is not strictly chronological.

Young Hattie Barnes and her mother, Maggie, are the central characters of *Sights Unseen*. The adult Hattie, years after the events she describes, re-creates her mother's illness and her own attempts at understanding it, as well as her feelings about it. Since she was a child at the time her mother began her recovery, she did not understand all that was going on, indeed having learned only much later of the electroconvulsive (electric shock) therapy which was crucial in her mother's successful treatment, although she reveals to readers in the novel's opening sentence both that this treatment occurred when she was twelve years old and that she had not known of it at the time. This sets up the contrast between the perceptions and understandings of the narrator at two important stages, that is, the adult telling of the knowledge, sometimes incomplete, of the child. Hattie generally speaks from the point of view of the child, but her adult voice sometimes intervenes, conjecturing or interpreting from the child's observations and the adult's greater knowledge. In fact, the adult Hattie (like her older brother) is a doctor and thus is able to write with special knowledge of both the mother's illness and her cure. The twofold perspective given by this combination of child and adult awareness is not unlike, in some ways, the complicating of perspectives through use of doubled or nested narrations which Gibbons had used in *A Virtuous Woman* and *A Cure for Dreams*, but it is more subtle and might be overlooked by some readers.

Sights Unseen is constructed of fifteen chapters which are divided into three major sections. These sections are not proportional in length, the first, containing eight chapters and concluding on page 115 (out of 223), comprising over half of the book. The second section contains three chapters and the third has four, both of these being much simpler in their narrative stream than the first, as well as being much shorter. The effect is in some ways as if the long first section sets up for readers the events of the second and third, while the second section relates a specific episode of the mother's madness and the final section brings it all to a climax by describing her treatment and recovery, the experiences for which all the rest of the novel had been preparing.

Although sections II and III are generally narrated in a chronological organization, the first and most complex section is not. It circles around several crucial events and gives dates, allowing readers to understand the story's time line. Among the important facts that readers learn in this section are that Maggie is cured in 1967, that she dies in a fall in 1982, that she causes an automobile accident in 1967, that she is pregnant in 1954 with Hattie, her younger child, and that her son is six years older than Hattie. The narrative describes some of these events and indicates their relationships to each other (the events of 1967 particularly, including the crucial six-weeklong manic episode), as well as telling a number of inserted stories which reveal the extent of Maggie's illness. Individual episodes, particularly the most important ones like the accident, which is responsible for the hospital confinement leading to Maggie's recovery, are returned to repeatedly and described in detail, and this very fact underscores their importance in the life of the family, as well as in Maggie's medical history.

Other episodes or situations of particular importance and thus emphasized either by repeated although not repetitious narration are the sexual relationship of Maggie and her husband and Freddy's experiences of his mother's strange behavior at his school. Both of these illustrate for the mystified children that their mother is not like other mothers and that their family life is abnormal. Both young people are deeply affected by their experiences and observations, and this impact is at the center of what the novel is about.

Of great importance about this first section is that it gives away the crucial facts that the mother will be cured as well as demonstrating how desperately important it is for the children, indeed for the entire family, that this happen. It also leads up to the depiction of the way she will be cured, in fact brings the reader to the brink of the decisive event that leads to the cure, the automobile accident in which Maggie injures an innocent stranger. But aside from indicating that the means of her recovery is electric shock treatment, it does not go into the nature of that treatment or its immediate effect on Maggie herself, nor does it say anything about the effect on the family of the hospitalization itself. This long opening section is about the illness itself and its effect on the family. Its length may have the effect of making the novel seem to be more about the illness than about the recovery, but another effect is that of underscoring the great need of both Maggie and her family for help, as well as setting up how that help finally comes.

Section II, chapters nine through eleven, centers on and describes at length one episode of Maggie's illness, a vacation at Hattie's grandfather's beach house, which occurs in 1963, four years before the automobile accident and Maggie's treatment. This narrative has not been prepared for in the long opening section and is yet one more, although a particularly important and graphic, example of Maggie's madness and its effects on her family. In this section, Hattie describes her own actions and feelings more fully than she had tended to do in the opening section, but otherwise it may be looked at as a continuation of the novel's first part.

Section III, chapters twelve through the story's conclusion in chapter fifteen, brings closure to the book. Like section II, it details its part of the novel in a generally chronological fashion, but its materials are more varied and cover more time. It opens with the sending of Maggie to the Duke Hospital for the treatment she so desperately needs, covers her therapy as well as family visits to her and depictions of her gradual change as her mental condition normalizes, and concludes with her return home. Where the opening of the novel—and of section I—had commented on the mother's electric shock therapy and the young Hattie's ignorance of it, the last lines of the book once again combine consideration of mother and daughter. However, here it is the adult Hattie who muses on her final coming to terms with all the memories she has dredged up in her narrative, both the pain caused by Maggie's illness and the joy brought when Hattie finally has a mother. Hattie has learned from retelling the story, and she presents herself as emotionally richer and more at peace as a result.

The novel's structure, then, is set up to give emphasis to several aspects of the story's tale, as well as to the emotional development of both central characters: the recovery from mental illness of the mother and the release from feelings of resentment and pain of the daughter. Along the way, understanding of the impact of mental illness upon a family has been depicted, as has the change in the behavior of the sick woman. The relationships of family members to each other as well, including the afflicted one, and the very special stresses added to all family relationships by the presence of mental incapacity are developed.

As mentioned earlier, Hattie's narration has the kind of doubling of vision familiar to Gibbons's readers from earlier novels. Here it is created by adult Hattie's telling of the story she had lived through as a child and her attempts at honestly re-creating what she then knew and understood (and did not understand), along with her greater knowledge and understanding as an adult. That she (along with her older brother) has become a doctor (8), a detail mentioned only twice, in passing, is significant, for the knowledge gained through her medical training explains her ability to include clinical information about the disease of manic depression, along with the nonmedical descriptions of Maggie's behavior and of the impact of it all upon the family. Readers might conjecture that the impetus for Freddy and Hattie to study medicine came from their observation of the almost magical effect upon their family's life of their mother's treatment.

Hattie's narrative, as already indicated, is only partly chronological. In part it operates by a kind of association, as when one episode suggests another which is similar to it in some way even though occurring at quite another time. Thus, the fifth chapter is framed by narratives regarding first Hattie's and then Freddy's births, although in fact Freddy is six years older than Hattie, and the eighth chapter touches on several incidents in which Maggie behaves inappropriately regarding the children's school activities.

CHARACTER DEVELOPMENT

Important characters in *Sights Unseen* may be classified into several groups: the two main female characters (Maggie and Hattie), one other significant female character (Pearl, the family's maid); two less important women (Aunt Menefee, Maggie's sister-in-law; and Miss Woodward, the grandfather's close woman friend); and important male characters (Freddy, Hattie's brother and Maggie's son; "my father"; and Mr. Barnes, Hattie's grandfather and Maggie's father-in-law). The most important of these are the central mother and daughter, subject of the narration and the narrator.

Maggie Barnes, middle-class wife and mother who has married, for love, into a wealthy and prominent family and who leads a life of privilege and comfort, is the object of her family's love and care. Everything in the family revolves around her needs, which are extreme and affect other family members in a variety of ways. She is much cherished by her husband and father-in-law, but her children have a more complicated relationship with her. They both resent the mental illness which so often incapacitates her and long for her to be the kind of mother that other children have.

Maggie's illness is called by its medical name, manic depression (currently it is more usually referred to as bipolar disorder), and her characterization is in large part the depiction of the way the disease affects her. Her behavior goes in cycles of normality, depression, and manic behavior, cycles which Hattie refers to as "her violently rotating condition" (62). In her normal or healthy periods, she is a beautiful, talented, and charming woman, but those sane times seem to grow less and less. Hattie sums up her illness by describing Maggie as "depressed almost always, and her sadness was fractured only by wild, delusional turns of mind, with brief periods of stability that were celebrated and remembered by the family as though they were spectacular occurrences, like total eclipses or meteor showers" (6–7). Her illness begins to manifest itself when she is a young adult, during the first year of her marriage (49) and is in full swing by the time her children are born. In fact, Hattie's conception is caused by her father's hope that a pregnancy will restore Maggie to a period of stability, as had happened when she was pregnant with Freddy. Hattie generalizes that depression seems to be Maggie's natural state, "and her sadness was fractured only by wild, delusional turns of mind" (the manic periods), and by the short-term periods of sanity (5). In these brief but dramatic periods of manic behavior, Maggie will not sleep, drinks heavily and makes incessant sexual demands upon her husband, goes on shopping orgies, and behaves in erratic, completely irrational and unpredictable ways that are both a worry and a humiliation to the family. Hattie's narrative spends much more time on the manic episodes than it does on either the periods of depression or the times of sanity, probably because these are the most dramatic and have the greatest impact upon the family.

The most important of the manic events is the automobile accident of 1967, in which, driving without a license, Maggie apparently intentionally runs down and injures a woman, a complete stranger, who she accuses of trying to steal her soul. It exemplifies the craziness of Maggie's logic when she is in this delusional state, although it is only one of a number of such episodes described. But other scenes add to this picture. Pearl, the family's cook and maid and Maggie's keeper, describes the first time she had seen Maggie: "I says, 'That woman is not right.' . . . She was just jerking . . . she was just slicing vegetables all over her nice countertop. Just ruining it" (38). The delusions often relate to prominent men who she believes are in love with her. They range from an attractive new minister who she is sure is not able to keep his eyes off her while he is in the pulpit (75) to a whole list of famous men who she knows from television or movies (22). Primary among these is Robert Kennedy, who she claims is in love with her and is coming to dinner, causing her to worry about what one should feed a Roman Catholic. She goes so far as to telephone a puzzled Catholic acquaintance and quiz her on the dietary requirements and customs of members of that faith. Remembering the requirement, then customary, of Catholics eating fish on Fridays, she decides that fish would be a safe menu item and then plans to feed him fresh flounder, which she will have sent from the beach. She even worries about what will happen to Ethel (Mrs. Kennedy) and "all those children" (23). All of this, of course, has absolutely no basis in fact, showing how very far she is from a normal reality when the manic compulsion is upon her.

Another example relates to Hattie's sixth birthday, of which there are no pictures, unlike all her other birthdays. Maggie had actually taken two rolls of film at the party and then, in a manic high, had been certain she could develop them. So she took the film out of the canisters, putting it into some solution she thought would develop the images on it (Hattie guesses that it might have been rubbing alcohol). Then she forgets about the film and goes off to do something else, but the film of course is ruined (87). Knowing about her manic states, Hattie imagines that perhaps in her delusion of being able to do anything, she decided to begin playing the piano or become a poet (87–88). She sees herself as capable of accomplishing anything she tries despite her lack of any experience, talent, or training. Examples could be multiplied, and Maggie's variety of crazy actions, as illustrated by Hattie's narrative, help the reader have some feeling for what it must be like to live with such a mentally incompetent person and thus have some understanding of the family's sense of isolation and desperation.

Somehow the family manages to cope with this irrational behavior, as well as with the depressed periods when Maggie sleeps much of the time and is emotionally absent from them. But when the woman she has injured with the car threatens to sue, they finally realize they must take action, leading to her time in the hospital affiliated with Duke University and the treatment she has so long needed. She is greatly changed by this treatment, perhaps not really cured but enabled with continuing care to live a normal life. She finally lives as what Hattie calls a "whole, rounded person," but the pity is that she has only fifteen years for this healthy life (11). Nevertheless, in this time she becomes the wife and mother her family had needed and longed for. In the last two pages of the novel, Hattie lovingly sums up her life and her strength, saying that she "stayed sane thanks to ample medication, particularly Miltown [a then widely used and popular prescription tranquilizer] and then lithium carbonate, psychotherapy, and sheer dint of will" (222), stressing the determination this took as well as her success in prevailing over her illness. From then on, Maggie, who had before hardly existed in a maternal role, attends all the important events of Hattie's life. Although the two of them never talk about their separateness during Hattie's first twelve years of life, Maggie demonstrates her love by her actions. And this is enough for Hattie, who at the end of the novel remembers with devotion her mother's "peaceful and smiling face . . . in the clear infinite light of October" (223).

Hattie's self-portrayal, through her narration, is as complex as that she gives her mother. And she, too, changes through the course of her experiences. Her change, however, is more understandable, more based in the reality most of Gibbons's readers know. Her story is that of the child who tries to comprehend and cope with her mother's erratic and frightening behavior while she longs for the maternal love which is unavailable to her. Her entire family revolves around her unpredictable mother, and her father's concentration on her mother's illness means that he, too, is largely not available to her. Her older brother, who had deeply resented her birth, becomes her companion and guide, and the family's maid serves as a kind of surrogate mother. But neither Freddy nor Pearl can compensate for what is lacking.

Hattie is a bright youngster but a lonely and puzzled one. She says that she "never abandoned the ideal of a mother" (5), even when her mother's behavior is most incomprehensible or frightening. She clings to the idea that she is worthy of having a mother and she believes that eventually she "would somehow have" the one who belonged to her (5). She writes of listening and watching the strange goings-on in the household and trying to make out what they mean. Like other of Gibbons's narrators, she is imaginative and able to reconstruct logical explanations for things she has observed. But perhaps the strongest impression left by her recounting of her youthful experiences is of her sadness, her longing for what she can not have. Over and over she says, "I wanted," "I longed for," and the like.

Even before she is born, there is alienation between Maggie and Hattie. Maggie, in her delusion, is certain that Hattie will be stillborn, and she then rejects her infant. It is only after the scolding intervention of her father-in-law that Maggie nurses her baby, but even that does not instantly create bonding between them. Even Hattie's name may be seen as indicative of the lack of relationship between them, for "Harriet" is selected by the child's father in memory of his deceased mother and "Pearl," her middle name, suggests the almost foster-mother relationship that will come to exist between the girl and the family's maid (32–33). Hattie, of course, does not remember that and is told many of the details of her infancy only later by Freddy.

The opening paragraph of the novel prepares for the disconnection between Hattie and her mother, as well as the deprivation she feels because of it. The adult Hattie, beginning her narrative, says, "Had I known my mother was being given electroconvulsive therapy while I was dressing for school on eight consecutive Monday mornings, I do not think I could have buttoned my blouses" (3). She is, she tells us, twelve years old at the time, considered too young to know what is going on, although readers learn later that she has been a horrified observer of her mother's erratic and even frightening behavior which leads to this treatment. But she also adds, almost immediately, that there is "a certain power in her healing" which the young Hattie does not understand, thus revealing almost immediately that the so far unnamed mother is to be cured (3). The young Hattie, then, is protected by her elders from participating in, or even knowing about, the attempts to cure her mother from the illness which has made Hattie's childhood so lonely and frightening. To the young Hattie, the change seems almost magical. The adult Hattie says that, as a child, she had worried about the lack of effect she has had upon her mother, regretting that love for her has not enabled Maggie to "will" herself to be well because of her daughter's need (4). The child, in her naïveté and lack of understanding, takes to herself some sense of guilt for her mother's long-continuing condition. After the cure, she also worries that her mother's illness and crazy behavior may return and that since love for Maggie's family has not been sufficient to make her healthy before the treatment, it may not be enough to keep her healthy afterward. She does also reveal to readers something of her mother's subsequent life as a healthy woman but does not say much about the relationship which then is able to develop between mother and daughter. The fact of Maggie's accidental death in a household fall, some years later, is also mentioned quite early, which gives emphasis to Hattie's sense of regret that her time with a healthy and nurturing mother is so short.

But before that, Hattie stresses the unfulfilled need for a mother which has colored her childhood and her lack of the maternal role model who might have taught her about becoming a woman. She sums up their changing relationship in these early pages by suggesting that they "caught each other just in time," as Hattie was just leaving childhood and becoming an adolescent (6), delaying her development so that the two of them could learn to know and love each other before she begins to become interested in boys and take other steps toward her own adulthood (7). These early pages, then, introduce both the young and the adult Hattie, suggest her place in her family and her changing connection with her mother, and begin to imply the dramatic nature of the change that Maggie's treatment will have, as well as on Hattie's development.

Perhaps the two major aspects of the young Hattie's view of her world are her puzzlement over her mother's behavior and her sense of isolation and alienation. Her puzzlement is obvious; because Maggie's mood swings are so extreme and her behavior so erratic and unpredictable, Hattie never knows what she will be like from day to day, almost from hour to hour. Hattie's isolation is almost equally obvious and pertains both to her relationship with other members of her family and to her lack of connection with people outside the family. Family members are so wrapped up in trying to control or conceal Maggie's illness that they have little energy to spend on the children. Hattie's father and grandfather, both of whom dote on Maggie, do not seem to understand how Maggie's manic-depressive illness is disrupting Hattie and Freddy's growing up or to comprehend the effects that their dysfunctional family life may have on these two young people. Only Pearl, the maid, attempts to give them comfort and nurturance and to explain to them their mother's condition. But however loving and wise, a maid cannot be an adequate substitute for the mother the children see and want to love and be loved by and yet who they know is not available to them emotionally.

Thus Hattie clings to Freddy, who after his initial resentment of her when she is an infant, becomes the one family member with whom she can honestly talk about her feelings and experiences. He is six years older than she and he has more experience and more understanding, but he, too, is just a youngster as they live through the years of Maggie's madness together. Although in many ways a typical boy, who teases his sister and has his own different unmet needs of his mother, he is still a teenager when Maggie's treatment occurs, so the assistance he can give to Hattie is limited. But at least Freddy and Pearl between them do manage to give Hattie some sense of stability and safety.

That Hattie does successfully come to a productive adulthood lacking the emotional and psychological scars her early family life might have given her is revealed in a number of varied ways. She is a doctor and the loving mother of two daughters (30). Like the fact of her profession, her motherhood is mentioned only by the way, to indicate that the lack of an early model of good mothering has not turned out to handicap her in this role. Whether she is married is not mentioned.

Finally there is the thoughtful and compassionate tone of her narrative. The adult Hattie is able to comprehend the viewpoints of quite varied participants in her story—her father, brother, grandfather, uncle and aunt, and Pearl, among them, but even including outsiders like the woman whom Maggie purposely and insanely injures in the 1967 automobile accident. She does not show the resentment or anger that might have been expected from a person who has had her childhood experiences. Throughout the novel, she maintains a generally objective narrative attitude, and from time to time, individual comments strengthen her kindly tone. The novel's close, as significant as its opening for the development of Hattie's character, is explicitly a statement of reconciliation. She comments that in retelling her mother's history and her own childhood experiences she has dredged up old memories that had previously been forgotten, memories of her youthful worrying and lack of understanding. She says that doing this has caused her to remember both "the pain her illness caused me and my inexplicable joy at her return to me" (222) and adds that both "forgiving and healing are true arts" (222–23) and that this recounting of her mother's story has enabled her to "forgive the past without reservation and heal myself" (223).

Healing can be physical, as Hattie knows well, having seen her mother's treatment and cure and undergone years of training to become a physician. But it can also be psychological and spiritual, and that is the sort of healing she is talking about here, a healing that has been brought about by remembering and retelling those memories. In recounting her mother's healing, she has enabled her own. And the last twenty lines of the novel, in an almost elegiac tone and in very poetic language, picture some images of the healed mother in her last years. The novel's close, then, concentrates on the peace and love that finally have come to this troubled family and to its narrator.

The remaining female character of real importance to Hattie's narrative is Pearl Wiggins, the family's maid of all sorts of work. Before her coming, the life of the family is chaotic. After she comes, a degree of order and peace is brought. Her coming to the family is her own doing, for she nominates and hires herself. While working for a man she holds in contempt, she hears about this troubled family and somehow knows intuitively that they need what she can bring them and that she can handle their troubles. Instead of applying for a position, which in fact does not even exist, she simply shows up at the house and tells Hattie's father what she will do for them and what she requires of them. She does not underestimate either her abilities or her worth. She announces that she will cook, clean, do washing and ironing, sew, shop, care for Freddy (Hattie is not born at this time), and watch over Maggie and keep her out of trouble. Her requirements are a "dependable automobile . . . something respectable" (and if Hattie's father can't afford to buy one right away, she'll be willing to drive the family's car in the meantime) and a salary of twenty dollars a week (although she is quite aware that the going rate at the time would be only half that [38–39]). She persuades Hattie's father to employ her by strength of will and character, and she does not disappoint them, for from this time forward life is easier for all members of the family.

But Pearl is more than a maid; she becomes a member of the family. She cares for Maggie and for Freddy, and then when Hattie is born, she cares for her. What explanations the children get of Maggie's behavior generally come from her, and she genuinely loves them all. When Maggie escapes her vigilance, takes the car, and causes the accident that injures an innocent woman, Pearl is consumed by guilt. She feels she has failed the family—she has, in her mind, apparently failed to do one of the tasks she had promised to do, in keeping Maggie safe, and disaster has been the result.

Usually, Pearl is very effective in controlling Maggie when the latter is in one of her manic periods. As Hattie points out, she has patience and stamina, both of which characteristics are essential, and she knows when to coax or soothe and when to be firm. As a character, she is in the tradition of other Southern black maids who are at the center of the functioning of the families they serve and are essential to the maturation of youngsters in those families. Several examples which come immediately to mind are Dilsey in William Faulkner's *The Sound and the Fury*, Calpurnia in Harper Lee's *To Kill a Mockingbird*, and Berenice in Carson McCullers's *The Member of the Wedding*. Some readers may feel that in this characterization Gibbons comes uncomfortably close to relying on the stereotype of the black "mammy."

Pearl's kitchen seems as much of a refuge to Hattie as does her own room, and a number of scenes show the two of them in that kitchen, with Pearl comforting Hattie or trying to help the child understand or cope with the odd goings-on of her family. When Hattie is very small, it is Pearl who picks her up and carries her about, "compensating for the infrequency of my mother's touch," as Hattie says (60). When she is pregnant for the first time, Freddy even teases the adult Hattie that although she has learned little about parenting from her own mother, she has learned from Pearl what she needs (69). Indeed, the entire family appears to recognize that in every real sense, Pearl is acting as Hattie's mother, and Hattie is grateful to her, calling her "my salvation" (70). After Maggie's treatment and return to normality, Pearl's duties in the family are lessened, as her responsibilities as nurse and keeper are no longer required and Maggie pronounces herself able to take over some of the general household duties. Nevertheless, Pearl remains an integral part of the family. Her force of character and personality and her gifts with people are emphasized by the high regard in which she is held by all the members of the family.

The other female characters, principally Miss Woodward and Aunt Menefee, are of much less importance to the novel, although both are interesting and both help to illustrate ways in which the extended Barnes family is unusual. Aunt Menefee is the wife of Hattie's father's brother and is a whiner and complainer who never quite understands or sympathizes with Maggie's illness or with the concern her brother-in-law and father-in-law have for her. She is mother to Hattie's cousins, and she is often on the fringes of the action. Miss Woodward, on the other hand, is a woman of some force. She is the sister-in-law of Mr. Barnes, Hattie's widowed grandfather, and becomes a significant other to him. She, too, is on the fringes of the family, but she is brighter than Aunt Menefee and allows her home to become a kind of refuge for Hattie's father when things are particularly hectic at home.

The three male characters who play important roles are Hattie's father, brother, and paternal grandfather. Freddy, as noted previously, is six years older than Hattie, and as a result he knows more of the history of the family and of Hattie herself. Therefore, he becomes a source of information for her. He teases her, as older brothers will, and consequently gets into trouble, particularly in the long section at the beach, but he also helps to keep her grounded. He assists her with her homework, explains family mysteries to her—as well as he can, for his knowledge, too, is imperfect—and he helps to give her the attention and stability her parents cannot. He is gifted but uses basketball as a physical release and an escape from the tensions in the family and is a mixture, according to Hattie, of "childhood innocence, adolescent confusion, and adult wisdom" (170). Like her, he becomes a doctor, and readers know that the relationship between the two remains strong, for Hattie several times remarks on telephone conversations the adult siblings have had.

Hattie's father, Frederick Barnes, is always referred to simply as "Father" or "my father." A weak man, he is less clearly characterized than either his son or, especially, his father. He loves his wife dearly, but he is unable to cope with her requirements or to maintain the emotional connections and life of his family. When Maggie's manic sexual demands overwhelm him, he flees to Miss Woodward's house to rest and find refuge. He allows his own father to interfere in his care for and support of his wife. Despite seeming ineffectual, he truly loves his wife, and he is so caught up in the problems he faces with her and his concern for her that he lacks the capability to be a father to his children, leaving them to the care of Pearl, although he has not even taken the initiative to find the help she offers. Lacking the love of a mother because of her mental illness, Hattie and Freddy also lack the love of a father.

A much more forceful and effective character, although a deeply flawed one, is Mr. Barnes, the children's paternal grandfather. He is a man of wealth and of powerful personality, a more benign tyrant than Ellen Foster's father but revealing some of the same patriarchal and demanding traits. He rules the family by both his power of character and his wealth. His relationship with Maggie is an odd one, for he loves his daughter-in-law deeply, more apparently than he loves his son or grandchildren. He gives her whatever she wants, and he interferes in her care, always being sure he knows what should be done. He demands that he be called "Mr. Barnes," even by his own grandchildren, revealing his insistence on his personal dignity. In her narrative, Hattie never refers to him in any way except by title and last name, abiding by the rule that he be addressed in that way by "anyone who was not in the position to call him Father" (34). His position in the community enables him to be what Hattie calls "a fixer" (13) who can, by a telephone call, keep reports on Maggie's public displays of her illness out of the newspapers. As a result of his power and his money, the family relies on him to put things right. Some of his habits, all in keeping with the dignity and formality of the name by which he is called, make him almost a comic character. He is unable to relax and unbend. Even at the beach house which he owns, he "walked the strand in gray pants and a starched white shirt, which he changed two or three times a day" (121). An old school gentleman, he illustrates the stiffness and authority of his type.

SETTING

Gibbons's usual North Carolina settings, the places of her own youth, appear again in *Sights Unseen*, this time more precisely identified than in earlier novels. The immediate family of Hattie and Maggie lives in the country near Rocky Mount, the town in which Gibbons went to high school. Hattie identifies their actual community as being Bend of the River Road and specifies that they live on a farm, but the activities of farming life are not referred to. Raleigh is the nearest city, and references to a Raleigh newspaper indicate that this is the urban area of importance to them. A state institution named for Dorothea Dix and what is always referred to simply as "Duke," a private university hospital, are also prominently mentioned, being the family's options for Maggie's treatment. Duke is their choice as the appropriate place for a woman of wealth and position to be sent, unlike the governmental establishment which treats charity cases.

As in Gibbons's other novels, little direct description is given of settings. The two exceptions are the beach setting for the novel's second section and the hospital in which Maggie is treated. However, even these places are described only so far as is necessary to enable readers to understand their effect on the characters. A rail on the balcony of the beach house, over which Hattie vomits, is of more significance than the beach itself, and the hospital is important not for what it looks like but for what takes place there, that is, Maggie's electroconvulsive treatments and her therapy. That all of this is in the South is less important to the action and characterizations than the Southern setting of Gibbons's other books.

THEMES

Several of the most important themes in *Sights Unseen* have already been touched on in the section on character development and need little more comment here. The most significant of these are themes relating to family and motherhood or mothering. Both of these are shown as process, from an early troubled state which changes to a more healthy condition as Maggie finally receives the treatment she needs to enable her to become a functioning mother and member of a functioning family. Her illness so preoccupies the other adult members of the family that they have no energies to maintain loving family relationships with each other. Additionally, Maggie is unable to fulfill her role as mother to her two young children, leaving them to the care of others, and because their father and grandfather are caught up in Maggie's condition and behavior, they are of little assistance to Freddy and Hattie. Thus, Gibbons portrays a family which does not operate as a healthy unit and which leaves its children largely to bring themselves up. If the Barneses had not been fortunate enough to have Pearl find them, Freddy and Hattie would have had essentially no adult supervision or nurturing.

This lack of adult oversight and care is shown to be painful and alienating to the youngsters as they are growing up, but Hattie's comments reveal her awareness that the effects on her could have been long lasting and serious. She remarks especially on her lack of a positive example, a role model, for her future life as a mother. She learns a great deal from Pearl, her surrogate mother, and finally, after Maggie's treatment and successful return to the family as a functioning wife and mother, she and Hattie are able to build a healthy—and healing—relationship with each other, one that gives Hattie the mothering for which she has yearned and which does give her a role model for her own later life.

Another theme, one typical of Gibbons, included in the novel is that of race, developed principally through the character of Pearl. As maid, she fills a stereotypical role in a white family, and as surrogate mother, as noted earlier, she resembles black female characters in other twentieth-century Southern novels. In the case of this novel, Pearl is also used explicitly although sparingly to stress a theme of racial equality. Hattie's parents, although not her grandfather, are firmly antiracist in their attitudes. In a time and place, the South of the 1960s, when black people were routinely addressed as "nigger" or, if they were male as "boy" and called by their first name only, no matter what their age or station in life, Hattie's father and mother insist on using language which treats African Americans with dignity and respect. For example, in the days of Maggie's illness, Pearl takes Hattie shopping for clothing, carrying with her "a check signed by my father and a well-worn note which read, 'Please let Miss Pearl Wiggins write this check against my account' " (215). This note not only suggests the trust given Pearl by the family in letting her fill in the appropriate amount for purchases, but it also gives her last as well as her first name, treating her as a full human being and equal.

One specific episode, occurring after Maggie is returned to health, illustrates the esteem given to Pearl within the immediate family. Mr. Barnes, in his characteristic thoughtless manner, refers insultingly to what he considers the "coddling" of Freddy by a "nigger cook." Maggie, who in the days of her illness had herself been coddled by Mr. Barnes and had been in many ways dependent on him, catches him up. She calmly tells him, "Pearl is not the so-called nigger cook. . . . She's part of this family, and I'll not have anybody, including you, talk about her that way" (210). Mr. Barnes had demeaned Pearl by relegating her to a servant's role and by using an offensive racial term. In so doing, he had turned her into an object, and one of little worth at that, but Maggie's rejoinder returns her to her rightful, and well-earned, place as a fully human and important part of the family. Her race doesn't matter, but her contribution does.

Finally, a theme of maturation is crucial to the novel. Hattie grows up, changing from an often puzzled, alienated, and lonely child into a mature professional woman and mother. On one level, the central subject of the novel is how she manages to do this, what dangers and problems lie in her path, and what aids her in overcoming them. Her initially dysfunctional family, her mentally ill mother, her lack of care and nurturing by her family—all these make her growing up difficult. The help and companionship of her older brother, the love of Pearl, the tutoring and encouragement by the two of them—all these help her reach puberty unspoiled and still with the potential to become a contributing adult. Her mother's recovery when she is twelve and the maternal love which she receives after that time make the rest of her maturing, not shown in the novel, a success. The contrast between the child Hattie who is one of the two major subjects of the novel and the mature, wise, and sensitive Hattie who relates her story illustrates both how difficult parts of her growing up have been and how successful she has been in overcoming her obstacles.

A PSYCHOLOGICAL READING OF *SIGHTS UNSEEN*

The term "psychoanalytical criticism" is often used very broadly to refer to literary studies which examine the motivations, often assumed to be unconscious and revealed through symbolism, which underlie and explain the behavior of characters. Similarly, the term "psychological fiction" is generally used to refer to fiction which emphasizes the interior lives, motivations, and feelings of its characters. According to these broad definitions, most fiction repays psychoanalytical criticism, and most novels can be considered to have some of the traits of psychological fiction. However, in the case of *Sights Unseen*, these terms may be used in an even more specific sense.

As noted earlier, mental illness and its treatment are central to this novel. Psychological examination of the motives and feelings of all characters, especially the two central women, Maggie and Hattie, are Gibbons's main interest in this book. Mother and daughter are psychologically presented, as the mother's illness impacts on both of them, Maggie from the inside as the sufferer from the disease and Hattie from the outside as one affected by her mother's condition. The novel follows Maggie through her period of mental illness, depicting her behavior and its effect on others, and then describes her treatment, as well as contrasting her behavior and relationships after with those before the treatment. From her later vantage point as a physician, Hattie is able to explain aspects of her mother's behavior that mystified and confused her at the time, as well as to describe the treatment itself and its effect on her mother as a patient. Thus, the theme of mental illness is developed from two viewpoints, that of the child who is affected by her mother's condition and that of the adult who has professional knowledge about it. Therefore, the psychology of the disease and its medical treatment also become subjects of the novel, and any full understanding of *Sights Unseen* must observe these aspects of its development.

Gibbons has acknowledged that this novel cut particularly close to home with her, for in it, as in *Ellen Foster*, she was coming to terms with some aspects of her troubled childhood, and here as well she examines her own illness, puzzling over what its effect could be on her own daughters. This insider's knowledge of the disease and its impact is doubly important here, for it comes in two forms. First, she has the experience of a daughter of a manic depressive. And more important, she has the intimate knowledge of the experience of one who lives with the illness and is the parent of children who must be puzzled and alienated, she thinks, by her sometimes odd behavior. In fact, she has said that in writing the novel she often imagined herself in the place of her own young daughters as she created the character of young Hattie. For these reasons, Gibbons is able to portray authentically and sympathetically the experiences of both Maggie and Hattie, although she has chosen to weight her presentation in the novel toward Hattie's point of view.

The most important presentation of mental illness and psychological condition in the novel is emotional, particularly the feelings of confusion, frustration, anger, and loss which consume family members. Most of our discussion has emphasized these emotional responses, and they are at the center of the book. They involve the characters as laypeople who are caught up in experiences which they cannot understand or control. However, Gibbons also relates objective information about the disease, making this a psychological novel which is somewhat different from most books called by this term. In this sense, it is somewhat similar to books like *The Snake Pit*, which examines the commitment of a woman to a mental hospital and her experiences and treatment there. Unlike *The Snake Pit*, *Sights Unseen* is not an expose and lacks any goal to point a finger at abuses within the mental health care system, but it does offer information about it. For example, the difference between state and private mental institutions is clearly indicated, at least as it relates to the question of which is the proper facility for a middle-class woman like Maggie. But Gibbons always consciously avoids propaganda.

The course of Maggie's treatment is followed in some detail in the later pages of the novel, just as the course of her illness had been depicted in its earlier portions. Her weekly electroconvulsive treatments and her resultant initial memory loss and gradual discovery through therapy of an ordinary life are described, some of this through Hattie's memory of visiting her in the Duke facility during her treatment and some of it from her later physician's knowledge of what it would have been like. Although electroshock treatments, widely used in the 1960s, were to be much attacked as their drawbacks and dangers became clear, Gibbons does not become involved in that controversy. Instead, she—and her novel—describe the treatment from the point of view of a patient and her family who were helped by them.

8

On the Occasion of My Last Afternoon
(1998)

Gibbons's sixth novel breaks new ground for her in a number of obvious ways, although careful readers will observe the presence of a number of characteristics and techniques familiar from earlier books. It most crucially resembles her earlier work by the use of first-person narrative by a strong female character and in being set in large part in her favorite North Carolina locations. In addition, it makes use of a number of Gibbons's familiar themes and character types. The central character, her father, and their African-American servant are most similar to characters in previous work, and themes of family, of motherhood, of marriage, and of both racial prejudice and equality stand out here as they have in other books by this author.

It is most strikingly different in being a historical novel, one set entirely in a past century and told mostly in chronological order. Although *A Cure for Dreams* and *Charms for the Easy Life* had made important use of time periods prior to the author's own experiences, both followed their depiction of those times to lead up to relatively recent events. Neither would be considered a historical novel in the usual understanding of that term. This latest work, however, has for its most important settings pre–Civil War Virginia and North Carolina before and during that war, and thus for the first time Gibbons has relied heavily upon historical research into events, not just into language and folk culture. This novel is also significantly longer than had been her earlier fiction, but like all of her work, it is much more intensely based upon characters than upon events.

PLOT AND NARRATIVE METHOD

Once again, Gibbons's basic plot is extremely simple. Her story covers the growing up of her central character on a Virginia plantation, the daughter of a loving and gentle mother and a tyrannically brutal father, her marriage to a Northern physician, their life together in North Carolina before and then during the Civil War as they tend wounded and dying soldiers and endure the hardships brought to the South by the fighting, her husband's early death from the exhaustion caused by the strain of his work, and her period of recovery from grief in the Boston of his family. Then, much as *A Cure for Dreams* had skipped over a number of years between its main story and the time of its narration, *On the Occasion of My Last Afternoon* jumps ahead to the turn of the twentieth century, as the narrator feels the approach of her own death and remembers back to the events and people who mattered most to her in her eventful early life. After the end of the war, the death of her husband, the successful growing up and happy marriages of her three daughters, and her return to the Raleigh where her happiest and most turbulent years had been spent, little happened that was of importance to her, and so time becomes foreshortened in her memories.

Emma Garnet Tate Lowell's narration, her recounting of her memories, is more ordered and orderly than that of earlier Gibbons storytellers. She does not skip around so much in time, and she does not rely so heavily on association of ideas or themes to guide her recollections. Twice, however, she does withhold important pieces of information, both times about the precise ways in which deaths occurred, until well after these events. Both revelations occur at the point in the narrative when they will have the most dramatic impact. The earlier is revealed when readers would need to have the information in order to understand behavior of Emma Garnet and her husband which would otherwise be inexplicable. This information about the manner of the death of Emma Garnet's older brother, well known and painful to her, has not been revealed, realistically enough since the pain caused her by the knowledge is so great that she would not wish to talk about it. But when it is publicly cast up to her, in a kind of ruthless social blackmail to which she reacts with humiliation and her husband with a protective fury, it is necessary that readers understand it in order to comprehend the event, and a flashback occurs to clarify.

A more lengthy withholding of information relates to the facts of the event in her father's boyhood which lies at the root of his anger and violent behavior and which also explains why Clarice, ostensibly his servant, is the only one who is able to exert any control over his violent and ugly behavior. That something terrible had occurred when he was a child is hinted at several times throughout the novel, and Emma Garnet clearly is puzzled at why he is the way he is. The question of his character, of what happened to him before the story begins, is finally answered near the end of the novel, being explained at the place in the chronology at which the narrator learns it. No hints had been given earlier that this event concerns the death of his mother. Only as the servant who has been with father and daughter throughout their lives is dying and is clearing her conscience and making peace with those she cares for, does she reveal to the narrator what she needs to know. Thus, Gibbons has used this mystery to build suspense and has attempted to create closure by its late revelation.

Like Gibbons's other novels, this one opens with a startling, even shocking sentence, one which leads readers into the horror which is to affect deeply the narrator's life and ways of looking at the world. *"I did not mean to kill the nigger!"* (1) cries the father of the then twelve-year-old protagonist, plunging readers into a horrible and crucial event, the earliest single momentous experience in her life. Her father is lying about his intent, having just slit the throat of a slave who had, he thought, been impudent to him as they were slaughtering a hog. This shocking scene accomplishes a number of functions, setting up the character of both the father and the society which he in some measure represents. It also sets up the maturing character and the beliefs of the narrator and the position in the family of the servant who is to be a kind of surrogate mother for her and a sort of moral conscience, standing against the evil of the father and the society. In the structure of the novel, this early scene is both an appropriate chronological beginning and a logical thematic beginning.

CHARACTER DEVELOPMENT

Gibbons's major characters here are—with one crucial exception—the immediate family by blood or marriage of a Southern woman: her father and mother, her elder sister and younger brother, and her husband. The critical exception is the free black woman who is part of her childhood household and follows her into her married life. The characters are vividly portrayed and present a great variety.

Emma Garnet Tate Lowell begins her life as a more realistic version of the type that had been portrayed by Margaret Mitchell in the Scarlett O'Hara of *Gone with the Wind*. Note that this is the romantic novel that Gibbons had treated so scornfully in *Charms for the Easy Life*, and her version here of the young woman being reared into Southern womanhood is far different from Mitchell's. Like Scarlett's, Emma Garnet's father is strongly patriarchal and sometimes violent, but he is a less benign and ultimately sympathetic character than Mr. O'Hara.

From the beginning, Emma Garnet's upbringing is intended to turn her into a sweet, beautiful, submissive, charming example of young Southern womanhood and especially to create in her a potential marriage prospect for a young man from some wealthy and aristocratic Virginia family. Emma Garnet, however, has no intention of becoming such a stereotyped person. Under the influence of her older brother and following her own inclinations, she develops a mind of her own, reacting against much of what she sees in her father. Where he is cruel and a racist, she accepts and loves black people and rejects the very concept of slavery. She is not interested in the proper young men whom her father wants her to attract, and when she does marry (much to his surprise, for he had given up on her ever finding a man who would take her!), the man she chooses is the last person he would have selected. A Southern girl from the plantation class and a slave-holding family, she marries a doctor from Boston who is from a famous family known for its abolitionist opinions—and she agrees with his principles.

Her strength of personality and her determination to live her own life by her own principles are empowered by the influences, both positive and negative, of several of the other characters. Positive influences are her bookish older brother, who encourages her love of reading, the black servant who protects her from some of the excesses of her father, and her gentle and loving but ineffectual mother. However, it is the negative influence of her father that has the strongest power over her development. The most dramatic and significant experience of her youth, which opens the novel, teaches her much about what she hates and rebels against. In that opening episode, set in approximately 1842, her father brutally kills one of his slaves. The gore of the scene, in which human and pig's blood are mixed and in which her father's indifferent cruelty to both victim and his family are demonstrated repeatedly, makes a very strong impression on the young girl. She already knows that her father is a liar, and she also knows that the slaves are individuals and have names and families. She is intuitively aware of the evils of slavery, and she loves and admires some of the black people as much as she already rejects the beliefs and actions of her father. Thus her eventual marriage to a man, who holds similar views, even though his opinions and background are anathema to her father, seems almost predictable.

Emma Garnet's marriage, during its early years, is idyllically happy, and she and her husband remain deeply in love until his untimely death. He brings out the best in her, helping her develop her abilities and understandings and even teaching her to be a very good amateur nurse, so that eventually they work side by side in caring for the wounded and dying in the bloody battles of the Civil War. Her strength, physical and emotional, and her courage are tested greatly during this period, and she surmounts every obstacle. She remains something of a mixture of stereotypically feminine and very untraditional abilities. She does not know how to cook anything except popcorn, as befits the daughter of a wealthy planter, but she is able to cleanse horrible wounds and comfort dying men. She is a loving mother, and she and her husband rear three daughters in whom they nurture their own love of learning and their principles of equality and humanity.

After her husband's death, Emma Garnet grieves deeply and for a time withdraws from the world, spending much of her time at his grave. But gradually she returns to life and takes an interest in what is going on about her. She continues to live by the principles which they had upheld together, feeling his influence always with her and devoting herself and her resources to a number of charities. This is the period of her life to which the novel's narration gives the least attention, summing it up quickly in preparation for the elegiac ending, which indicates (as had the title, of course) that her death is upon her. She stresses, in her last afternoon, that she is glad to have relived the past through all the memories she has just recounted, but that she is now ready to follow her husband in death.

The most compelling character in the novel is Samuel P. Goodman Tate, Emma Garnet's father. He is a collection of contradictions, a tyrannical patriarch of his family who is cruel to his children from his wish to bring them up to be satisfactory members of the Southern aristocracy which he has joined by hard work and force of will. He is an owner of slaves who sees them as less than human because of their race and condition of servitude, as unworthy even of having their individual identities recognized, and yet he was rescued from a horrible childhood situation and then reared by a free black woman. He came from poverty, the son of an ignorant and brutal father who forced him to kill his own mother, but he has become the wealthy landowner of a fine plantation and is a self-taught scholar of classical language and literature. An outsider, one who originally was a victim of the Southern aristocratic system, he is an avid defender of that system, one of the hotheads who call for secession and war, for the defense of slavery and the rights of the Southern states before war comes, and who stubbornly upholds that system all through the war. A self-taught lover of art and collector of fine paintings, he has no respect for the possessions of others, destroying a valuable carpet owned by his son-in-law in a fit of anger. His own collection has been acquired by visiting "Panic" sales of paintings owned by men in financial straits; Emma Garnet calls it "legalized pillage" (23). He has been elected to two terms in the Virginia legislature and is "known all over Virginia to be an honest, upright, hearty, and earnest Episcopalian" (2), but within his family he is a tyrant and a bully.

When his plantation, Seven Oaks, is taken over by the Northern army near the end of the Civil War, he descends on his son-in-law and daughter in North Carolina, taking over their parlor, removing their possessions and installing his own, announcing that he will now reside there, and demanding that he be served at his convenience. He doesn't even recognize the fact that the household he has invaded is also suffering from the effects of the war, that his son-in-law and daughter are exhausting themselves in caring for wounded soldiers, and that provisions are almost impossible to procure. His own comfort and safety are all that matter to him, and he even endangers the safety of his unwilling host and hostess by writing inflammatory letters to the newspapers. His arrogant intent is to rule this household as he had long ruled his own.

Throughout his life, he is accustomed to dominate those around him. He fails twice in his own family, losing his oldest children. He intends for his son Whately, a talented, bright, and sensitive boy, to become a man in his own image and is successful only in that Whately loves learning as much as his father. But his sensitivity seems weak to the father, and he succeeds only in driving Whately away, which leads ultimately to the boy's early and horrid death. He alienates his daughter, Emma Garnet, who has neither the desire nor the ability to become the kind of empty-headed, submissive, charming Southern belle that he wants to make her. Her fortunate marriage is a happy escape for her, and she is happy to cut all ties with her father. He seems more successful with his younger daughter, Maureen, turning her into the kind of young woman who he thinks will be most able to make a good marriage, but then he is never satisfied with her suitors and ends up keeping her for himself, to run his household and become an old maid. His younger sons, sent off to work for him in Italy, are encouraged by Emma Garnet to escape both his ensnarement and the horrors of the war by staying abroad, and thus they, too, escape him. The result of his arrogant and cruel behavior is that he drives away from him all members of his family except for his long-suffering wife. Fittingly, he dies unrepentant, still not recognizing or caring about the brutality of his treatment of others or the stupid one-sidedness of his views of life. He cares only for himself, and others are merely puppets to him.

The novel's opening scene perfectly illustrates all his worst traits, places him in a violent situation for which he refuses to take any responsibility. Having killed a slave, he is so indifferent to his victim's death that he does not even recognize that this man had an individual identity. Clarice, the free black woman who has brought him up and who is the only person who has any control over his actions, is the one to insist that the victim be identified, who sends for his wife who is a slave on a neighboring plantation, and who oversees the death ritual by which the rest of the slaves touch his toes in order to protect them from being haunted by his ghost (7–15). It is meaningless to him that, as Clarice puts it, *"He had a name and it was Jacob"* (17), and it is equally unimportant that his action angers the rest of the slaves, reminding the twelve-year-old Emma Garnet of all the horror stories she has heard of the Nat Turner slave rebellion (1). He makes no move toward keeping peace with his slaves, and it is only the efforts and manipulation of Clarice that prevent further violence. He bullies his way through life with no concern for the existence of others, and this bloody opening episode illustrates all that very well.

One other incident from Emma Garnet's childhood will serve to illustrate his strange view of child rearing. Reading in a newspaper that two men are to be executed in Williamsburg with all sorts of surrounding festivities, he insists that his entire family go on a kind of holiday to observe. The family is entertained by a local celebrity whose home overlooks the green where the double hanging will occur, and he insists that they be well positioned up front in the crowd to watch the execution. In his usual fashion, he rides roughshod over the wishes of his wife, who does not even want him to read to the younger children the newspaper accounts of the crime for which the two men are to be executed. Instead, in the family prayers which he leads, he requests "blessings on the excursion" (93) and points out that execution teaches lessons about the consequences of sin. He entices the younger boys by promising them all sorts of fun at the circus which will follow the hangings. In this episode, instead of being the perpetrator of violence he is an eager observer, and his infliction of its horrors upon his gentle wife and young children is an interesting revelation of his methods of hardening them.

As noted earlier, one of the most important pieces of information about this paradoxical man is revealed only after his death. When Clarice, the black woman who had been the heart of the family for many years, is dying, she finally reveals to Emma Garnet the secret about his youth. Emma Garnet calls it "the hidden truth" (238). As a child, he had been forced by his own alcoholic and abusive father to shoot his mother, help his father bury her, and then guard her shallow grave from wild dogs. Clarice took him in and reared him, becoming a foster mother to him but never succeeding in comforting him or helping him recover from the psychological damage done him at such a young age. Now, at her own death, she wants Emma Garnet to be able to understand why he had become so harsh and uncaring, tracing his character development—his brutality, his tenacity, his courage, his hatred and anger—to this pivotal event. Like Clarice who withheld this information throughout his and her own lifetime, Emma Garnet withholds it until the place in her narrative at which she learns it (238–40).

Mr. Tate's wife is as gentle and sensitive as he is brutal and uncaring. She is another example in Gibbons's fiction of a woman who "marries down" in class or station. She had come from a prominent and socially elite Savannah family which had fallen on hard financial times (45), so that her marriage to a wealthy newcomer rescued them from poverty. She patiently suffers her lot as the wife of a man who, in her daughter's opinion, is totally unworthy of her. She bears his children and attempts to rear them to be good people, runs his household, and fulfills her role as an aristocratic hostess with distinction. Her unhappiness with her situation is shown by her periodic escapes to visit other families whose lives are more placid and refined than that of Seven Oaks. She is absent from the plantation on just such a visit, what she calls "an escape holiday" (6), during the opening scene in which Jacob is killed, for she hates the blood and the stench of the annual hog butchering. Her other "escape" is into the migraine headaches which she frequently suffers. Emma Garnet stresses her gentle sadness and her attempts to be cheerful. In marrying and escaping from Seven Oaks and her father, Emma Garnet's only regret is that she cannot take her mother with her, rescuing her from her hideous marriage. She promises to return for her, but then is caught up in her own new and happy life, and her mother dies still in the power of her controlling husband. In spare language but with heart-felt emotion, Emma Garnet sums up her sense of guilt by saying, "I am ashamed" (52). Adored by her daughter, Mrs. Tate never becomes much more than a gentle and idealized presence in the background of the novel, for her characterization lacks the vigor of that of her husband.

Of the six children of this marriage, the three younger boys are not very important. As children, they are in the background and figure very little in narrative. As young adults, they are abroad and are mentioned only in regard to Emma Garnet's hopes that they will stay there, escaping both their father and the war. Whately, the oldest child, is closest to Emma Garnet and the most influential during her growing up, and his loss leaves her with a scar which never heals. Maureen is not very important during the early parts of the novel, for as girls she and Emma Garnet are so different that they hardly relate to each other. Her importance comes later on, near the end of the war, when the two, now adult women who have matured through suffering, draw close to each other.

Whately is much like his mother in some ways, having her gentleness and kindness. But he also has his father's love of learning, and his escape from the attempts of his father to harden him and create in him what he appears to see as masculinity is to go to Washington College (now Washington and Lee University) in Lexington, Virginia. Like Emma Garnet, he rejects his father's ways of thinking and sees blacks as people, not undifferentiated laboring objects. He teaches Emma Garnet, and she receives much of her education from him. She credits him with giving her a love for and appreciation of the usefulness of the English language.

After the incident at the hog butchering, the children's father, still denying any responsibility for Jacob's death, turns his attention to his oldest children. Whately especially bears the brunt of his anger. Emma Garnet, although she, too, dissatisfies him by not being the type of young woman he wants, is allowed to remain in the household, but Whately is exiled, which, however, merely confirms a foregone conclusion. From the time he was twelve, "the age of accountability" (72), he had said that he would not inherit Seven Oaks or live there. He states that he does not wish to be a slave owner. Angered then, his father had pointed a gun at his son and forced the boy to admit what his father was convinced of, that Whately was a weakling. The bargain reached as a result of Whately's rejection of his father's heritage is that the father promises to pay for his college education as long as he promises not to seek that education in the North. When Whately arrives home from college in December, deeply troubled, he confesses that he is responsible for the pregnancy of a barmaid (78), shameful both because of the sexual act involved and the social status of the woman. The father finally sends him away, bitterly angry, but does see to it that he has an opportunity to support himself in Charleston.

Humiliated and depressed, Whately remains his gentle self in saying good-bye to the two members of the household who are dearest to him, his mother and Emma Garnet. He gives his sister some of his most loved books and leaves her a note recommending to her the writers and books he most admires. He understands, she thinks, that in his absence the books will have to replace him as her refuge and comfort. And it is only a little later that he dies, alone and in partially self-inflicted pain, the victim of his own mistake and of his father's cruelty. He had contracted a sexually transmitted disease in the sexual act that impregnated the barmaid, and his attempts to treat his symptoms have mutilated his body, the physical description being horrifying (83). The physical excess that brought about his downfall is less venal than those sins which his father has repeatedly committed, but his weakness and sensitivity, so different from his father's brutal and arrogant strength, lead to this early and pathetic death. Emma Garnet's loving and sad epitaph is that he was "just a boy who loved his books" (84).

The remaining member of Emma Garnet's birth family to play an important role in the novel's action is her sister Maureen. Younger than Emma Garnet and having little in common with her in interests or temperament, Maureen is generally ignored by her older sister during their youth. She seems negligible to Emma Garnet, but she is a gem to her father. She has all the characteristics of the aristocratic Southern woman which he values and which he thinks will enable her to marry well. She is pretty, charming, and willing to work to be attractive. She takes pride in her appearance and intends to find an appropriate young landowner and become his wife and hostess. Emma Garnet later sums up her sister by saying that "she conformed like a well-fitted satin glove to Father's vision of resplendent young ladyhood" and lists the characteristics that make Maureen both charming and shallow (134). Emma Garnet can only scorn her younger sister who knows so well how to charm and manipulate men.

After their mother's death, Maureen becomes imprisoned in her situation as her father's beloved and servant. Ironically, and sadly for her, she has conformed so well to his ideal that she is prevented by him from ever living up to his original goal for her, a fine marriage which will increase his own prestige. Instead, she is kept on as his hostess and companion, maturing past the age of first beauty and marriageability. Emma Garnet, now married and living in North Carolina, understands quite well what is happening but has never had enough sympathy for her younger sister to care very much, though she does feel some pity.

During most of the war years, the sisters' relationship is maintained only through letters, and it is only in 1864, near the end of the war when Seven Oaks is occupied by the Northern army and Maureen and their father come to Raleigh that Emma Garnet really understands how her sister has grown and comes to value her for the strong woman she is. Her beauty is now gone (206) and she is tired to exhaustion, having suffered mistreatment from her father much like that meted out to their mother. But she is brave and strong, and she has managed to endure. In the last days of the war, when Emma Garnet's home is filled with wounded men, Maureen organizes activities and keeps Emma Garnet going (247). She is a failure as a nurse, although she tries, because she cannot stand the sight of blood, but she does everything she can to be of help. She grieves deeply over Clarice's death, feeling guilt and shame for not having valued her rightly during her childhood (232). While a widowed Emma Garnet is safely in Boston, she lives through the troubles of the early postwar years, and eventually she succeeds in the noble goal of establishing a home for women and orphans (268). It is in this "charitable house" where, as alone as Whately had been, she dies (271), but she has made her life productive and useful. At the end, Emma Garnet grieves deeply for her.

Also a member of Emma Garnet's family, although not by blood, is Clarice, the free black woman who in his horrible childhood had rescued Mr. Tate and brought him up, protecting and to some degree controlling him. Free blacks, it should be noted, were not uncommon in the period and, in fact, sometimes even owned slaves themselves, a fact which figures significantly in Gibbons's plot. As Mr. Tate grows up and eventually prospers, she remains with him, and when the novel opens, she is the family's cook and chief house servant. However, it is immediately clear that she has a very special relationship with her employer, as she is the only one who is not afraid of him or can in any way control his actions or his rages. The opening episode establishes that. She insists that he tell her the name of the slave he has killed, and does not listen to his blustering excuses for both the deed and his ignorance of the man's identity.

Clarice essentially takes control at that point, finding out who the man was, seeing to it that her employer cleans himself up, and in effect publicly humiliating him before the rest of his slaves. She sees to the respectful treatment of Jacob's body and questions the eyewitnesses about how the tragic act had actually occurred. She keeps the peace, leading the other slaves in paying their respects and in the ritual of touching Jacob's toes. Most important, perhaps, she causes an only slightly puzzled Emma Garnet to behave submissively to her, indicating her own authority over members of the white slave-owning family. Slave rebellion, a specter raised in the novel's opening page, is averted by her wise and perceptive behavior (1–15).

Clarice's loyalty, first to Mr. Tate and then to Emma Garnet, might seem to place her uncomfortably in the stereotype of the black "mammy," but that loyalty is not a sentimental affection for and admiration of her betters. It seems to be based on her feelings of responsibility for the boy she rescued because of pity and regret, perhaps even guilt, that she had not been able to save him from becoming a man who carries on his own father's thoughtless brutality. She finally leaves Mr. Tate, going with Emma Garnet at the time of her marriage, leaving him sputtering that she must return to him. She never does, and he has no hold on her that can force her to do so. She remains with Emma Garnet, and here, too, responsibility and guilt would seem to be motivating factors, as explained by her deathbed revelations. A very wise woman, she understands that just as Mr. Tate had been deeply wounded by his childhood experience, so had Emma Garnet been wounded by her upbringing at his hands. Finally, when he is dead and she is dying, she feels released from her obligation, taken on voluntarily, to care for him and keep his secret. And thus in her wish to help Emma Garnet understand why and how he had become what he was, she tells his secret.

Clarice is an abolitionist at heart, but a realistic one. She understands her situation as a free black in the pre–Civil War South and knows that she must live carefully and will be truly safe only when in the employ and thus under the protection of a white man. Throughout the novel she protects other African Americans when she can do so, and her keeping the peace after the killing of Jacob is motivated by her desire to avert an uprising which would be as dangerous to the slaves as it would be to the white family. Even though they might have succeeded in killing Mr. Tate, their revolt would be brutally put down and they would suffer as much as he. As Emma Garnet points out, her abolitionist goals do not extend to altering history by ridding the world of slavery. Rather, she simply wants to help members of both black and white races live with grace and dignity in the circumstances in which they find themselves. And Emma Garnet stresses the dignity with which Clarice lives.

Clarice keeps another guilty secret. In this case, however, the secret is kept from those it most closely affects but it is Emma Garnet's and her husband's secret as well as Clarice's, and readers know about it all along. Once again secrecy is maintained from what she considers to be sufficiently good, even urgent, motives, but once again Clarice comes to believe she has wronged others by not revealing the truth. When Emma Garnet marries and moves with her new husband to North Carolina, Clarice, who as a free black woman had the right to choose her own fate, goes with her. That much is public knowledge. What is not known is that Emma Garnet's husband, an abolitionist by conviction, purchases the freedom of three of the Tate slaves, an assistant cook to Clarice, a housemaid, and a butler. The former slaves in question, and everyone else, are allowed to believe that they are now owned by Clarice, a deceit thought necessary to protect the now free servants, as well as Emma Garnet and her husband. Emma Garnet points out that it was not unusual for blacks to own each other in that area, and that trouble might have been caused for all of them if it were thought that Emma Garnet's new household contained more than one free black. They are treated just as they would have been had they been known to be free, being given good pay, comfortable housing inside the main family dwelling, and good food (36).

On her deathbed, however, Clarice can hold the secret no longer. She summons the three servants and bluntly tells them, "The three of you—I don't own you. Nobody don't" (236) and then proceeds to lecture them on what they should now do. She insists that they first help prepare Emma Garnet to manage without them and then gives them a second kind of freedom, her permission to go wherever they want. The three, who have for so long been unaware of their actual legal status, are indignant at the deception, regretting both their lost years and, in one case, the lack of foresight to save money, but Clarice insists that they blame her and not Emma Garnet, repeating that it was her fault, her idea (237). In fact, Emma Garnet seems also deeply affected by the revelation, as having the truth come out removes the weight of guilt which she has repressed and rationalized over the years. Clarice's revelations thus free her in a different way both from that in which they free the servants and from that in which she is freed by learning the truth about her father. To the end, Clarice is a benevolent force, even despite the deceptions she has practiced.

Emma Garnet's husband, a doctor, a northerner, and an abolitionist, represents everything her father hates. Marrying him is an escape both from a repressive household in which slavery and abuse are ever present to a life in which she can live by the principles she has adopted in defiance of her father. Quincy represents everything she loves. In fact, some readers may find him too good to be true, an idealized portrait of the perfect husband and lover. He certainly rebuts the criticism of Gibbons that her male characters are uniformly portraits of villains.

Their courtship and marriage are skipped over, except for a brief description of their meeting at a dance and Emma Garnet's (and her mother's) immediate recognition of his quality (46). Quincy Lowell is the bearer of a very distinctively New England name, for he is a member of a historically prominent family of Boston aristocrats as his last name indicates, and his first name is also current in the region. His parents are by birth members of an elite, unlike Emma Garnet's father who only pretends to that station. The one meeting between the two sets of parents is disastrous, a dinner party in which Mr. Tate openly insults Mrs. Lowell, abusing both her gentility and their views on human equality. A brand-new medical school graduate, Quincy has come south to take up a position at a Raleigh hospital, meeting Emma Garnet on his way there, and from the beginning attempting to live by his egalitarian principles in the slave-owning South. He delays his arrival at his new position to establish a school and pharmacy in Virginia for free blacks (54), but he has the tact to deflect potential criticism when he can. For example, when asked whether in view of his " 'leanings,' " presumably his political convictions, he would be able to treat Rebel soldiers, if it came to war, as his " 'own kind,' " he replies that " 'everyone is my own kind' " (54), thus escaping criticism and even earning admiration. At a dinner party soon after their arrival in Raleigh, when a snobbish and opinionated woman quizzes Emma Garnet about her mother's rumored gentle care of her slaves, Emma Garnet disregards Quincy's warning signal and plainly reveals her own feelings. Although he had tried to hint that his young wife act with the same discretion that he was accustomed to show, he supports her heavily and then risks the ostracism he had been trying to avoid by his own plain speech (61).

Quincy always supports and encourages Emma Garnet. When war comes, he is overwhelmed by his work in caring for the multitudes of wounded and dying who are brought by train to Raleigh. He trains Emma Garnet to become a competent nurse, and the two of them work side by side throughout the war, finally turning their home into an added medical facility, even performing surgeries on top of their grand piano. Readers see him, of course, through Emma Garnet's eyes as she much later is remembering their happy marriage. Before 1859 and the gathering of the clouds of war, their marriage is idyllic. They have three daughters, on whom they dote and whom they rear in their own principles. After the coming of the war, the marriage remains as strong and devoted, but they become a team, working together and sharing their sufferings. Quincy's birthday gift to Emma Garnet in 1861, the year of the coming of the war, is emblematic. It is a silver brooch, engraved by himself by using a medical tool with the year and her initials. When pressed, he explains that the silver came from the dental work of a dead patient and that the date is meant to commemorate not the beginning of the war but the year in which " 'I hereby graduate you from medical school' " (185–86). He shows his love for her, recognizes the skills she has learned, and acknowledges the material deprivations and the suffering surrounding them in one emblematic gift.

During the war, Quincy's position in Raleigh might easily have become very difficult. He refuses to accept military rank (167), thus abiding by his rejection of the Southern slave system, but he gladly accepts the command of a military hospital. Throughout the war, he serves those who need his care without any discrimination, but he does so without expressing his political opinions as much as is possible.

When the war finally ends, he is a broken man, having worked himself into exhaustion. He expresses only the desire to " 'go home' " (259), meaning to go north. It is on the train ride to Boston that he unexpectedly and peacefully dies, having "slipped away as gently as he had lived" (260). Emma Garnet has presented him as truly an ideal man, and she mourns him deeply. She buries him in his native Boston, where she says she will eventually rest beside him. After a period of grief, she comes to feel his presence his urging her to return to the kind of work they would have done together had he lived—charitable work of caring for those who need help—and so she returns to Raleigh to spend the rest of her life (267–68). In her loving memory she tries to live up to what he helped her become and to continue his care for the helpless. His fine example and teaching live on long after his death.

The three important male characters, Mr. Tate, Whately, and Quincy, contrast markedly with each other. Mr. Tate represents one extreme of masculinity, that of brutal and arrogant strength, whereas Whately and Quincy both differ in being sensitive and principled, aware of and caring about the needs of others. However, Whately lacks the strength Quincy has in abundance, and his ineffectuality leads to his destruction. Mr. Tate dies in rage and alienation, while Whately dies in isolation and pain. Only Quincy dies a meaningful death, having sacrificed his health for the good of others, and thus it is suitable that his influence should continue after him in the work of his widow.

SETTING

Like Gibbons's other novels, *On the Occasion of My Last Afternoon* is set in the South. However, as this is a historical novel, its setting in time is as important as its placement. The South of the nineteenth century, with depiction of both pre- and postwar life but centering on the years of the war is in fact the principal subject of this book. More attention is given to what prepares for war than to what follows, but the war itself and its accompanying suffering, not on the battlefield but in a military hospital and in a home, is probably what makes the greatest impression on most readers.

Gibbons's two primary settings in place are Virginia—a plantation and the town of Williamsburg—and North Carolina—a hospital and a home in Raleigh. The Virginia setting is used before the war begins, as Emma Garnet is growing up there, and ceases to be a significant focus of action when she marries and leaves with her new husband for North Carolina. Seven Oaks, the plantation her father has created in the aristocratic image of his ambitions, is shown as a place with both great wealth and luxury for the white family and great suffering and hard labor for the black slaves. The slave system is clearly what allows this plantation, and the plantation system in general, to survive and be prosperous. Even as children, Whately and Emma Garnet understand the inequality and cruelty, as well as the absurdity, of the system on which their prosperity is based. The opening scene, in which Mr. Tate kills a slave, makes clear that to him the pig (which he says he was intending to slaughter) and Jacob (whom he claims to have killed accidentally) were little different in their value to him. Both were expendable, and except for the public shame which attaches to his act, he feels no more emotion for the killing of a black human being than for the butchering of a domesticated animal.

The unjust system which was a cause of the eventual coming of war is clearly and horribly depicted in this opening scene.

The home itself is a mansion, filled with art and learning, for Mr. Tate has brought to it great paintings and he has learned to read classical literature and loves it deeply. The contradictions of the man echo those of the system: beauty and gentility and love of culture based on a foundation of the forced labor of others who are kept ignorant and have no rights at all. Gibbons does not explicitly state all these things, although some are expressed through Emma Garnet's comments on her feelings about it all at the time. They are made clear through the life of the family and the character and behavior of its patriarch.

Williamsburg is the setting for the episode of the execution which the children's father insists that the family attend. He sees it as an edifying and educational experience for his children, one which will teach them about the consequences of crime—seeming totally unaware that his own brutal and inhuman behavior is no better than that of the men who are executed. But it is also to be a treat for the children, as the hanging will be followed by a circus, and there will be all sorts of entertainment for the children, such as clowns and freaks and other amusing performances. Here, too, the scene is a mixture of gentility and brutality. There is the dinner party given by the Tates' host family and the lovely and civilized arrangement of the town, with its church and government buildings, but there is also the erection of the scaffold on the central green and the gathering of the holiday crowd, thirsty for the violence of a legal killing and eager to enjoy itself at all the festivities surrounding it. The sixth chapter of the novel follows the family from Mr. Tate's first reading about the approaching execution through their visit and experience of it all. Ironies abound, and the family completes its holiday in general disappointment. Williamsburg and some social attitudes of the time—and these were typical not only of the South—are shown both as both comical and brutal.

In the chapter which immediately follows the description of the trip to Williamsburg, Emma Garnet turns to her life in Raleigh. The contrast is surely intentional. After just having described a kind of hell, she opens with, "We had Eden" (109), her summary of the life she and Quincy lived, soon with their three daughters, after settling in Raleigh. It is not that North Carolina has a society that is any more just than that of Virginia, for she quickly shows that prejudice toward slaves and white people who value them is just as great in the society of comfortable white Raleigh people. What is different is that she is now in a marriage that enables her quietly to deny the principles of the society. They employ a free African-American builder to work on their new home, and they fill it with their own books, including, of course, Quincy's medical books and those treasured volumes which Emma Garnet has smuggled out of Seven Oaks (112). They create there the peace which never could exist in the plantation, and they are able to do this because they are intentionally but quietly subverting the rules of the society in which they live. Quincy always insists on caring for black people as tenderly as he cares for whites, and there are only free servants in the household, although this fact is kept secret, for the safety of all concerned.

When the war comes, Gibbons depicts the suffering of wounded soldiers and of the civilians who try to tend them. The military hospital at which he now works, and eventually the family home, are filled with battle victims, and the difficulties of caring for them, especially in light of the blockade which often made it impossible to get needed drugs and other supplies, are sharply depicted. Even the use of maggots to assist in the care of infections helps to make real the nineteenth-century medical practices, as well as the horrors of the situation.

A careful reader with some historical knowledge can follow the course of the war, at least that part of it fought in the northeastern portion of the battle areas, through the names of the battles from which wounded soldiers are brought to Raleigh to be treated by Quincy and Emma Garnet. But the military aspects of the war, except as they produced gore and suffering, are not Gibbons's subject. Neither, aside from the institution of slavery as a cause of the fighting, are political events. The Emancipation Proclamation, coming near the end of the fighting and freeing those slaves in areas held by the Confederacy, is mentioned with scorn, for both Clarice and Emma Garnet understand well that it "frees" only those slaves who are not in areas where it may be enforced (244). As a secret sympathizer with the North although herself a Southerner, Emma Garnet expresses enmity for only two Northern generals, men famous for atrocities committed upon civilians under their control. These are "Beast" Butler, commander of an occupied New Orleans, and General Sherman, invader of Georgia and burner of Atlanta (257). And in the postwar Reconstruction period, she comments on the stupidity of attempting to change the South by destroying it (264) and mentions, in passing and in scorn, an illiterate note from a member of the newly organized Ku Klux Klan, ordering her to stop educating former slaves (270).

THEMES

A number of Gibbons's familiar themes reappear in *On the Occasion of My Last Afternoon*. The themes of family, motherhood, and marriage are developed here through Emma Garnet's experiences of, first a dysfunctional birth family but loving mother trapped in an abusive marriage and then, second, her own happy marriage with a tender husband and her success as a sensitive mother. Gibbons's development of these themes has been illustrated above in the examinations of character and plot.

Another theme of interest which has been observed also in earlier novels is that of medicine and healing. The characters in this novel, however, are more conventionally involved in medicine, as Quincy is a professionally trained physician, unlike Charlie Kate of *Charms for the Easy Life*, and Emma Garnet, as a woman and his helper, fulfills the conventional woman's role of nurse. The focus is on the kinds of horrible medical situations the Lowells meet as a result of the carnage of war, not on the kinds of folk and traditional therapies that the earlier women had merged with their more conventional methods. But Gibbons's continuing interest in the theme of healing, shown prominently in *Charms for the Easy Life* and *Sights Unseen*, where the healing is mental rather than purely physical, is obvious in this latest novel.

The theme of racial prejudice and discrimination, appearing consistently in Gibbons's work, is present and important here also. In this novel alone, she grapples with the topic of slavery, the "peculiar institution" characterizing her area of the country in the period of the novel. She depicts Southern society before the war, the society glamorized by novels like Margaret Mitchell's *Gone with the Wind*, the film of which she had attacked in *Charms for the Easy Life*, as shot through with inconsistencies. It is a cultured and luxurious society, but it is built on the foundation of slave labor which enables the wealthy to experience lives of great privilege. Like Mark Train, who had satirically given the ship which founders in *The Adventures of Huckleberry Finn* the name of *Sir Walter Scott*, she associates the decadent society she is attacking with the romantic views of the early nineteenth-century author, who idealized medieval Britain and whose views were often adopted by mid-nineteenth-century American Southerners defending their way of life. One of Gibbons's most explicit associations of Scott with an idea of the South which she rejects comes relatively early in the novel, when Emma Garnet is defending her plain speaking. She says, "Making an honest account is what, everything, I want to do and must do. Although I am a Southern woman, my life has not been cast in that romantic ideal of Scott's" (62). And much later, as the war is coming upon them, she comments on the rejection by women—who are mothers, wives, daughters, and sisters of men who will be expected to fight and die—of the romantic posturing of the men. She explicitly points out that the quotations from *Ivanhoe* have ceased, that these women now prefer living family members to heroes who have died valiantly, like knights of old. The reality of war has overcome the romantic ideals of the prewar times.

Denying the romantic idealization of the gentler aspects of the old South, Gibbons—through Emma Garnet—depicts the horrors of slavery. In part this depiction comes through the brutality of the treatment of slaves, such as the terrible and pointless killing which opens the book. In part it comes through the contradictions of Mr. Tate's character, in which brutality mingles with love of culture, paralleling the contradictions of a society of privilege based on the horrors of slavery. In part it comes through the sympathetic portrayal of Clarice, the strongest and wisest character in the novel. In part it comes through the rejection by Emma Garnet and Quincy of slavery and their refusal to participate in the institution by being slave owners. Most sadly it comes through the deception of three actually freed slaves who are led, for practical reasons, to believe that they are still slaves and through the guilt felt most strongly by Clarice, another African American, and by Quincy and Emma Garnet, two privileged whites, for the deception. Against their will, the Lowells have been persuaded to participate in the institution they hate, for they must know that if the three were aware of their actual status as freed people they would not remain in servitude, however well paid. The tentacles of slavery and its attractive ability to manipulate even well-meaning abolitionists make clear its corrupting power on those in positions of control.

It is primarily through the depiction of slavery that the evils of racial discrimination are shown here. One small detail, however, is telling. A society which enslaves one group on the basis of its skin color does not hesitate to employ other forms of stereotyping and belittling. Anti-Semitism is also taken for granted, and at a dinner table discussion in Williamsburg, during the family trip for the execution, talk revolves around Jewish power and obnoxiousness in Europe and in New York. Clearly none of the people at the table has any real experience with actual Jews, and their willingness to label all of them in broad generalizations is different in effect but not really in type from their scorn for and dehumanization of African Americans.

A FEMINIST READING OF *ON THE OCCASION OF MY LAST AFTERNOON*

Our two previous feminist readings, of *A Virtuous Woman* (see chapter 4) and *Charms for the Easy Life* (see chapter 6), both dealt with novels set in the twentieth century. With *On the Occasion of My Last Afternoon*, we are moving back into the nineteenth century and into a culture in which women's lives were strongly controlled by the expectations of an aristocratic society. A feminist examination of such a novel of necessity looks at the ways in which a woman either gives in to those expectations and is molded by or refuses to abide by them. In observing the experiences of women in such a society and showing how they are affected by the patriarchal power to which they are subject, such a feminist analysis seeks to enable readers to come to increased understanding of the past and, at the same time, of the effects of the past upon the present.

In looking at Emma Garnet and her narrative, a feminist critic will observe that her life falls into three periods. The first is a time of subjugation to a brutally patriarchal father who rules with total power over his family. Her mother is a traditional woman, a lovely, gentle, tender woman who accepts her subjection to her husband, with her only rebellion being her escapes to neighboring plantations, her headaches, and her occasional soft protests. Emma Garnet's model for the conventional woman, much as she loves her mother, is such that she can see her only as a victim needing to be rescued. That she fails to rescue her is a cause for lasting guilt. Her father's model repulses her and causes her to reject the beliefs and customs of her society. Thus she gains strength and independence, and in refusing to grow up to be what her father wishes, she becomes an autonomous individual, one who sees the world through perceptive eyes and who insists on living by what she has learned, not by the rules others would seek to teach her.

The second period of her life includes her years of marriage to Quincy Lowell, first in idyllic happiness as wife and mother before the war and then in suffering and pain but in fulfilling work alongside him during the war. She is fortunate in having found a husband whose beliefs match her own and who has an integrity matching hers. During the narrative

of this portion of her life, the focus tends to be on her experience and
activity, and so her development is not so much examined as taken for
granted. She is revealed to have great strength and courage, a fine example for other women.

The third period of Emma Garnet's experience comprises her years of
widowhood and occurs after the war is over. First, her grief over her
husband's death, occurring on his way home to Boston, and her beginning recovery in that city are shown. She gradually ceases visiting
Quincy's grave constantly and becomes involved in becoming something
of an authority on Southern cooking, her first real attempts at independent action, at doing something purely on her own. In this period, she
concludes another part of her life in conventional female roles: she is no
longer a wife, but she is still a mother. It is only after her daughters have
been educated and married, remaining to live in the North whose customs and beliefs most reflect those in which they have been reared, that
she returns home to Raleigh and takes up life as an independent agent.
However, it should be noted that she both returns home and takes up
charity work as the result of a kind of vision of Quincy, in which he
urges her to continue to live by their joint values and to carry on the
work they had begun together (267–68). Nevertheless, the many charitable works which she undertakes are possible only because of the competence and authority she has achieved and the strong and autonomous
woman she has become. In her singleness, much though she mourns and
misses her husband, she finds great fulfillment. As a feminist model for
her times, she is as worthy as Charlie Kate had been in hers.

Bibliography

WORKS BY KAYE GIBBONS

Charms for the Easy Life. New York: Putnam, 1993; Bard, 1998.
A Cure for Dreams. Chapel Hill, NC: Algonquin Books, 1991.
Ellen Foster. Chapel Hill, NC: Algonquin Books, 1987.
On the Occasion of My Last Afternoon. New York: Putnam, 1998.
Sights Unseen. New York: Putnam, 1995; Avon, 1996.
A Virtuous Woman. Chapel Hill, NC: Algonquin Books, 1989.

WORKS ABOUT KAYE GIBBONS

Bennett, Barbara. *Comic Visions, Female Voices: Contemporary Women Novelists and Southern Humor*. Baton Rouge: Louisiana State UP, 1998.

Gibbons, Kaye. "The First Grade, Jesus, and the Hollyberry Family." In *Southern Selves: From Mark Twain and Eudora Welty to Maya Angelou and Kaye Gibbons*. Ed. James H. Watkins. New York: Vintage Books, 1998. 70–82.

Gretlund, Jan Nordby. " 'In My Own Style': An Interview with Kaye Gibbons." *South Atlantic Review* 65.4 (Fall 2000): 132–54.

Guinn, Matthew. *After Southern Modernism: Fiction of the Contemporary South*. Jackson: Mississippi UP, 2000. 57–90.

Hoffert, Barbara. "Writers' Renaissance in North Carolina." *Library Journal* 1 Nov. 1989: 44–48.

Jordan, Shirley Marie. "Kaye Gibbons." In *Broken Silences: Interviews with Black and White Women Writers*. New Brunswick: Rutgers UP, 1993. 65–82.

Lewis, Nancy. "Kaye Gibbons: Her Full-Time Women." In *Southern Writers at Century's End*. Ed. Jeffrey J. Folks. Lexington: UP of Kentucky, 1997. 112–22.

Malinowski, Jamie. "Dedicated Lines." *New Yorker* 25 Dec. 1995/1 Jan. 1996: 46.

Manuel, John. "Clear Vision: An Interview with Kaye Gibbons." Chapel Hill, NC: Algonquin Books, n.d. Rept. *Spectator* 19 July–25 July 1990: 1–12.

Mason, Julian. "Kaye Gibbons." In *Contemporary Fiction Writers of the South: A Bio-Biographical Sourcebook*. Ed. Joseph Flora and Robert Bain. Westport, CT: Greenwood Press, 1993. 156–68.

O'Briant, Don. "Book Signing." *Atlanta Constitution* 20 Sept. 1995: Dixie Living 3M.

———. "Civil War Tale New for Gibbons." *Milwaukee Journal Sentinel* 17 June 1998: Cue 4.

Powell, Dannye Romine. *Parting the Curtains: Interviews with Southern Writers*. Winston-Salem, NC: Blair, 1994. 115–33.

Summer, Bob. "PW Interviews: Kaye Gibbons." *Publishers Weekly* 8 Feb. 1993: 60–61.

CRITICISM AND REVIEWS OF NOVELS

Ellen Foster

Barnes, Linda Adams. "Telling Yourself into Existence: The Fiction of Kaye Gibbons." *Tennessee Philological Bulleting* 30 (1993): 28–35.

Groover, Kristina K. "Re-Visioning the Wilderness: *Adventures of Huckleberry Finn* and *Ellen Foster*. *Southern Quarterly* 37.3–4 (Spring-Summer 1999): 187–97.

Makowsky, Veronica. " 'The Only Hard Part Was the Food': Recipes for Self-Nurture in Kaye Gibbons's Novels." *Southern Quarterly* 30.2–3 (Winter-Spring 1992): 103–12.

Monteith, Sharon. "Between Girls: Kaye Gibbons' *Ellen Foster* and Friendship as a Monologic Formulation." *Journal of American Studies* 33.1 (April 1999): 45–64.

Munafo, Giavanna. " 'Colored Biscuits': Reconstructing Whiteness and the Boundaries of 'Home' in Kaye Gibbons's *Ellen Foster*." In *Women, America, and Movement: Narratives of Relocation*. Ed. Susan Roberson. Columbia: U of Missouri P, 1998. 38–61.

Watts, Linda. "Stories Told by Their Survivors (and Other Sins of Memory): Survivor Guilt in Kaye Gibbons's *Ellen Foster*." In *The World Is Our Culture: Society and Culture in Contemporary Southern Writing*. Ed. Jeffrey J. Folks and Nancy Summers. Lexington: UP of Kentucky, 2000. 220–31.

A Virtuous Woman

Chandler, Marilyn. "Limited Partnership." *Women's Review of Books* 6 July 1989: 21.

Kaveney, Roz. "Making Themselves Over." *Times Literary Supplement* 15 Sept. 1989: 998.

Souris, Stephen. "Kaye Gibbons's *A Virtuous Woman*: A Bakhtinian/Iserian Analysis of Conspicuous Agreement." *Southern Studies: An Interdisciplinary Journal of the South* 3.2 (Summer 1992): 99–115.

A Cure for Dreams

Branan, Tonita. "Women and 'The Gift for Gab': Revisionary Strategies in *A Cure for Dreams*." *Southern Literary Journal* 26.2 (Spring 1994): 90–101.

Humphreys, Josephine. "Within the Marriage, A Secret Life." *Los Angeles Times Book Review* 19 May 1991: 13.

McKee, Kathryn. "Simply Talking: Women and Language in Kaye Gibbons's *A Cure for Dreams*." *Southern Quarterly* 34.4 (Summer 1997): 98–106.

Peat, Isie. "Books about the South." *Southern Living* 26.6 (June 1991): 86.

Tate, Linda. *A Southern Weave of Women: Fiction of the Contemporary South*. Athens and London: Georgia UP, 1994.

Charms for the Easy Life

McCauley, Stephen. " 'He's Gone. Go Start the Coffee.' " *New York Times Book Review* 11 April 1991: 9.

Sather, Kathryn. "Southern Story with a Bite." *Montreal Gazette* 15 May 1993: K4.

Summer, Bob. "PW Interviews: Kaye Gibbons." *Publisher's Weekly* 8 Feb. 1993: 60–61.

Thompson, James. "Man-Taming Granny: Charlie Kate Birch Is a Feminist's Ideal Grandmother." *Book World The World & I* 8.9 (Sept. 1993): 349–53.

Sights Unseen

Harris, Michael. "Scenes—and Skeletons—of a Troubled Southern Family." *Los Angeles Times* 9 Oct. 1995: E5.

Kenney, Michael. "An Author Confronts Her Inner Demons." *Boston Globe* 20 Sept. 1995: Living 77.

O'Briant, Don. "Book Signing." *Atlanta Constitution* 10 Sept. 1995: Dixie Living 3M.

Wolcott, James. "Crazy for You." *New Yorker* 21 Aug. 1995: 115–16.

On the Occasion of My Last Afternoon

Fisher, Jane. "On the Occasion of My Last Afternoon by Kaye Gibbons." *America* 180 (2 Jan. 1999): 16.

Harrison, Kathryn. "Tara It Ain't." *New York Times* 19 July 1998: 7.12.

McKay, Mary A. "Gray Ghosts: Civil War and Remembrance through the Eyes of Another; Compelling Kaye Gibbons Character." *Times-Picayune* 16 Aug. 1998: D6.

Szatmary, Peter. "A Slaveowner's Daughter: Kay Gibbons Outlines a Family's Civil War." *Houston Chronicle* 28 June 1998: Zest 26.

Treadway, Jessica. "Old Times There Are Not Forgotten." *Boston Globe* 31 May 1998: N3.

Wagner-Martin, Linda. "Kaye Gibbons' Achievement in On the Occasion of My Last Afternoon." *Notes on Contemporary Literature* 29.3 (May 1999): 3–5.

Index

About the Author

MARY JEAN DEMARR is Professor Emerita of English and Women's Studies at Indiana State University. She is the author of two previous Critical Companions, *Barbara Kingsolver* (1999) and *Colleen McCullough* (1996). She is also co-author of *The Adolescent in the American Novel Since 1960*.

Critical Companions to Popular Contemporary Writers
First Series—*also available on CD-ROM*